The Culture o

The Culture of Capital

Nicky Allt

Liverpool University Press

First published 2008 by
Liverpool University Press
4 Cambridge Street
Liverpool, L69 7ZU

British Library Cataloguing-in-Publication Data
A British Library CIP Record is available

ISBN 978-1-84631-127-7

Typeset in Jansen Text and Hypatia Display by Koinonia, Manchester
Printed and bound in the European Community
by Bell and Bain Ltd, Glasgow

Contents

⌗

Acknowledgements

To Allts and Fagans everywhere who gave me my culture, and to the Liverpool Mafia who only say YES to a 'YESMAN' – they'll never give you your real Scouse stories, brethren.

To Anthony Cond and Robin Bloxsidge at LUP for their patience, and boss little Joseph Connor Allt for the three-year diamond glint in his eye.

They all laugh at us, they all mock at us; they all say our days are numbered...

Sintroduction

Nicky Allt

※

And so 'Roll up, roll up for the magical mystery tour, step right this way' as the most famous, suited and booted band of all time once said. And the irony is: Liverpool is probably the least tarted-up and formally dressed place in the whole of Great Blighty. We're talking about a place where a tie often feels like a deadening collar a boss pins on his subservient workers, and an open-necked shirt and an ocean breeze carrying salted scent of the Mersey is forever life affirming. 2008 eh... Who'd a' thought a riotously belligerent place like Liverpool would come this far in time, and stranger still, be given something of an award for its cocky, rebellious-like nature? The Tories wanted it 'sorted', or off the map twice in the last century, at one time training British naval guns on its shores and then economically starving the place to almost standstill. But we remain on British soil and of British birth (most of us), so welcome.

While I'm at the reception stage, may I also extend a warm Northern welcome to all you visiting Capital of Culturites who might be having a dekko at this book inside WH Smiths or Waterstones in Liverpool city centre; if you are, then close the cover and go and pay for the thing immediately you hovering, bookstore door-hinge, cos this is me, a real-life, doused-in-Scouse Liverpudlian who had to get up off his bum and battle to get this thing in print. I tried the deaf-eared Culture Company, like a 1001 others of Mersey skin, but they blanked my emails, letters and phone calls after no doubt marking me down as just another bad scally with a brazen idea. The powers that be may think it's their 'showcasing shindig' and absolute novel way of securing outside investment, but in my mind's eye it's the residents do, and they can *do* as they see fit.

Similarly, if you're scanning these pages and you're a local Joey or Mary Ellen then do the do and the book as you please. Take an hour reading it in the shop. It's your city and as far as I'm concerned you can act whatever way like in it... well... except maybe walk the streets singing the praises of London and Manchester while telling everybody that sushi tastes better than fish and chips, and that marvellous Margaret Thatcher and gorgeous Gary Neville should be made King and Queen of England – it's still against the law for brother and sister to marry you see. And if you're going to be the 'weakest link' by playing to the Anne Robinson shoplifting stereotype, then be quick and don't be obvious, big brother is watching. The security tag is on page 54 by the way.

Concerning the shoplifting theory she lazily went on about, the thing I've struggled to work out is why oh why didn't she come here to get her fucking face lifted then? Try putting some of your Big Bag of Cash (BBC) money back into your home city you be-freckled-faced, Crosby moose, because not to go with a cheap Rodney Street skin-drag... that I'll never understand. Er, and another thing while I'm on, I make no bones about writing my thoughts in layman English and in native Scouse cos, bottom line, it's why I'm here. Anyway, culture thingy or no culture thingy, it's where I'm at and forever will be... Amen. The esteemed Bill Shankly logic that men of education trying to keep ordinary people in the dark will say 'men of avarice' instead of 'men who are greedy' will forever be a motto I push a pen by. He was a great man Shankly, a man of the people, 110% Scottish Scouse and one of us. Oh yeah, and he didn't need any facelift.

In my view Liverpool belongs to its people: Irish Scouse, Welsh Scouse, Scottish Scouse, English Scouse, European and African Scouse and Asian and Caribbean Scouse; always has, always will. As a native, all you have to do in cowboy town is put your head above the parapet, step up to the mantle and take pure' n' utter ferocious aim. For reasons of equity and home-comforts we seem to have gone all safe-as-houses and overcoat-comfy lately; taking aim from the plush leather settee and local pub lounge, and *saying* instead of *doing*, and face it, *doing* is what we were always known for. Funny the way this city always shows up large or *larger* in times of adversity. Believe me, now that people are more materially possessed, we should be kicking-off and driving our tasty station-wagons up to the doors of 10 Downing Street and the local town hall more than ever before. Now we've got a more upwardly mobile chance to change things for the long-term good, we should be bang-at-it! So let's get bang at it in Culture year.

We were always nonconformist and forever-confrontational, and glory-be-to-god for that. But again, believe me when I say that never has there been a more urgent time when YOUR city needs YOU and your nonconformist input. Just clock what they do with your council-tax money, how they clean your mintiest streets and how they organize your Cultural 'Liberal' Party in this grand old year of 2008. Then don't say something – DO SOMETHING! Even if it's dancing naked down Scotland Road with your knickers in the air! Believe me, it's your party… if you want it to be.

With me in these pages are other born and bred Scousers who checked in with some fine individual pieces about how they view life on the once razor-sharp banks of the River Mersey. Razor in wit, sharpening to flit; we laughed and we travelled, then laughed some more. We were always a city with movement, transience and of an immigrant nature; so while welcoming you visiting Culturites, I'd also like to extend a warm gold-sovereign-of-a-welcome to the new generations of Asians, Africans and other Eastern Europeans (mainly Poles) who reside here. I say, bring them all on, we could do with some hungry, fresh new Scousers. When I say fresh, I mean not too bogged down with the slimy, backhander politics of today, and being scared of who you might upset in case they might be a future rung on the ladder to individual success. Liverpool people were never scared of speaking out, but I have to admit I was surprised when a few people who were originally up for doing a few words for this Mersey Memo eventually bottled out when they knew the chosen subject and how I'd like it told. The yuppification of the whole of Great Britain seems to have finally reached Liverpool's rebellious streets, as upwardly mobile Scouse social climbers finally throw a dice at the Capitalist 'You Too Can Be a Winner' game. Play safe, grease palms and egos, and you too might 'get on'.

Even though we still have some of the most socially deprived pockets on these isles, I just wish more people would take to those streets to bang a few drums for their own downtrodden areas, instead of being living-room and pub-lounge apathetic, or proudly turning the other cheek. But as a lot of the older bedrock neighbourhoods of Liverpool get economically and culturally blanked, sometimes it seems like we've become too cool, lazy or proud to rebel against the powers that blank us. While I'm on about getting culturally blanked, how do you define a bad scally? Heavy local accent, lived a bit of life, doesn't play the doff-yer-cap game? That was the filtered down S.P. that whittled its way to my lughole through the Liverpool grapevine – Scouser-phobic Divvies!

In this politically correct world we live in, where tokenism beats individualism hands down, I might've been wiser phoning up using a Polish accent, offering a blag Polish immigrant story. I'd have stood a far better chance of getting-it-on and getting listened to then wouldn't I? Anyway, Robin and Anthony at the University Press were good enough to lend me another lughole by listening to my plea about the non-participation of Scousers in all things 2008, and about how Liverpool people need to empower themselves today and step right up, and again, step right this way.

Look, Liverpool's not about telling the outsiders how lovely we are, and Liverpool doesn't mean playing the green and pleasant land game. No, it's about talking differently, acting differently and actively wanting to be different. It's about change for the good, for the new, and against the lazy nature of familiarity breeds contempt. It's why we have a culture in the first place, why I'm writing this and why we're here in 2008. Same is safe and boring, same is cap-in-hand and yielding, same is doffing the cap in reverence to green and pleasant land.

Right, here we go, you listening? Then shout it: Liverpool is about the General Transport Strike of 1911 which brought the city to a stand-still, when 66,000 seamen, dockers and transport workers told slave-driving, anti-union employers 'go fuck yerself', and the closest thing to an English revolution took place between the army, the police and the working people of Liverpool. Intense battles and riots lasted the whole summer of 1911, with hundreds of casualties on both sides. Liverpool's defiant militancy and show of working solidarity was unprecedented at the time (would be today), sending a message to the ruling Tory classes that still reverberates around Whitehall whenever they need an example of 'People Power' to wag a finger at. On a lighter note: it's also about the best comedian in the land, Ken Dodd, maybe having a million pound stashed away in his Knotty Ash loft, after not paying his battle-axe on time. All that money and he couldn't go private to get his railings fixed? And Militant Labour taking on the Tories, again, in the mid-1980s. (Whatever your thoughts at least we would not be dictated to.) Or Liverpool's youth inventing the enormous football 'casual scene', after travelling to Europe to watch their teams in the mid-seventies and bringing back clothes that made them stand out like beamed-down spacemen on the English terraces (till the rest of Same-old Blighty joined in).

Liverpool is about young scallies and old dockers who sing and dance all night in the pub, and girls pushing prams who should still be in prams themselves. With rusted ships, blabbing lips and raucous quips, is it any wonder the place can feel edgy. Liverpool is warring gangsters who like to think they're top of the tree but in reality they're just roaming gangs of Armani-wearing James Cagneys reaching for Al Capone's darkened star. As well, it's about great boxers who become pub owners and taxi drivers, and ex-footballers who enjoy a weed at pub stay-behinds in the South End of the city. It's about North End haulage drivers who've smuggled more illegal duty in one year than the Royal Family did in a century or two of cut and swathe.

And listen, don't tell me about clean parks and tall glass buildings; tell me about muddy Sunday League footy fields where it can 'go off big time'! And empty dock warehouses where dodgy deals are made. As for million-pound flats, let me Kwik-fit you a million flat tyre stories regarding speed bumps the size of Bechers Brook and huge, gaping sink holes the size of Jordan's bra cup. Talking culture an' all that, take a moment to think about the other side of John Lennon, the one that gave Yoko Ono a slap; and we're not talking domestic violence here, no, we're talking about someone who definitely needed a backhander every time she attempted to sing... well, didn't she? And Paul McCartney singing 'Band in the Nick' after he got sent to jail for toking the gear; and Ringo losing the plot in California, years after grabbing Pete Best's job and coming into a right few quid; and George having to fight off another mad Scouser who burgled his house to have a bit of a gab about life and god an' all that. Talk about the edgy, talk about the naughty, talk about Liverpool with its dirty, shitty boots on.

Talk about the healthy arrogance of wanting to be different, of not wanting to be the same as the rest of England, the place that has ignored our hard-accented call year after year after year. Today's regeneration is English imported and, as usual, so are the suits who are carrying the plans and spending all the wonga. 'Government of the day's' plans for redevelopment are always old hat ideas brought in from other English towns. Liverpool is about resilience and its own entrepreneurial way of working things out. Look out to sea always. Look inland only if you want a leg of lamb! Enjoy Liverpool, Culturites, and ask questions about Dock Road lament and dockside dissent because the underbelly is where the real story comes from, where Number One hits first get strummed and where famous football songs first get aired. Ask the local Scousers about Spring Heel Jack and Jack the Ripper, and Hitler's brother and the Bizzies, and go to Greaty Market on a Saturday afternoon and be truly entertained. Buy under-the-counter goods and Marks and Spencer seconds, and be enthralled by the stall owner who'll tell you they're better than the ones in the shop.

Make it your Culturite duty to ask about the last twenty to thirty years of social exclusion from the London plan, and then about the suburbs' exclusion from the city's Cultural plan. Visit the Royal Court, Lighthouse, Olympia and other community theatres, and not just the nicely funded ones in your face and in town. Go shopping in Bootle New Strand and see real Scousers at work and at play. Drink in boozers that never close, but are never open. Go to Knowsley's Kirkby, Huyton and Halewood districts and meet real Scousers who got reeled out. Check out Skelmersdale and Winsford (Skem has roundabouts to die for and Winsford has a boss sweetshop) because there are more real Scousers out in those hinterlands. But be careful, they're a bit near the old woollyback strongholds of Wigan and Crewe for my liking, and you don't want to go catching what they've got, do you? See, if you get lost on Skem's roundabouts for three months, and panic because you're starving, and you eventually make the wrong turn into Wigan and you're unsure of what awaits you, then you're a dead-man-walking cos I'm talking: bad 'aye-up-lad' accents, bad market town threads and bad streaky-gelled-hairdos, oh yeah, and fellers who marry whippets and ferrets that catch then cook yer' tea!

Liverpool is about punching way-above its weight, and football teams and supporters that think, sing and win big. Yeah, you've got Lacosted boys and orange-faced, pyjama-clad girls in number on the streets, but you've also got suited and booted wannabes who drink in posh hostelries, while dreaming about becoming Speke's version of Brad Pitt or Fazakerley's answer to Angelina Jolie. Liverpool's wannabes are the funniest in truth. They keep the tanning salon owners' outlook sunny, the designer clobber shopowners well-dressed, and are a never-ending source for local stick-givers. Sat there acting the 'big truck', all drinking five-pound tipples, while places like the Casa and Ned Kelly's have got a lovely two-pound pint just around the corner. Got to be seen in the right gaffs haven't we darlings!

Taking the Gerry Rafferty song as lead, it's like hundreds of overpaid clowns to the left of me, thousands of jokers to the right, here I am, stuck in the middle with the few. If ever a city has got something of a 'battle of two cultures' going on, especially at this moment, then believe me, Liverpool's is the funniest and most pronounced. Thinking back to when I first came up with the idea to write this book, I was going to call it *The Battle of Two Cultures*, till the suits did the usual

confetti job with the 99-million pound budget, and the title, like a John
Conteh right hook, slammed me full in the face. It seems some of our
younger artists who live and write in the city think likewise about 2008.
As a social comment, here's a verse or two from a song called *Mersey
Market Tits-up* by a new Liverpool band called The Tiny Crocodiles.

Mersey Market Tits-up

If yer' checking out the city
Yeah yeah, it's sitting pretty
But watch out for the fallout
Cos there ain't no bottomless kitty

They're doin' the L1 and L2's up
But jibbin' out the higher number
And when those brand new shops lie empty
That's when you'll see the lumber.

Concerning where our money has been thrown about – house brick
size salaries apart, that is – here's a poem about applying a coat of Dulux
gloss over the city centre, and the trumpeting of fancy new shops in the
run up to 2008. Written by a Liverpool street poet calling himself A
friend of Steve McQueen, I instantly liked its natural bluntness.

Two Cultures

Here's the Paradise One project with its new designer shops
An' another brand-spanking dealers' club where the music never stops
It's all glossy fronts and 4x4s and tasty leather seats
While purple bins with holes burnt-in line minty fuckin' streets

We've got Met quarters and wag daughters and flats that cost a packet
And Culture bums with company chums all wearing Council jackets
And Ringo's comin' and Macca's strummin' so go and get the ale in
Cos there's Liver clocks and miles of docks but not a ship to fuckin'
    sail in

They've started the next penthouses and named them Pierhead 42
Steven Gerrard's bought straight off-the-plan so Arteta wants one too
They're the first to cost a million with glorious views across the sea
Not to mention Mathew Street debacles and arsehole blags to you an'
    me

There's cappuccino girls and latte boys all killing to be the faces
Dropping names and playing games while seen in the right places
With Baby Creams and celeb dreams and a gay quarter always heavin'
We'll wine and dine on Sun headlines about Scousers always thievin'

An' pricey shops where big name drops may likely lower cost
But don't walk in with bottoms tucked in in a two-piece blue Lacoste
Cos Cricket's here and Garlands Queer and Baby Blue's a thumpin'
With ramped-up roads an' loads of holes me car just keeps on jumpin'

Though councillors gloat and spend our dough on superficial things
    that gleam
An' footballers and their orange wives play out a movie called Obscene
It's all mansions and castles and things that dazzle and knickers that
    show no seam
Meanwhile Kensington, Dingle and mothers single are left at home to
    dream.

Oh the staggering hypocrisy of phoney-ism that just won't go away
While Dixie sleeps and Shankly weeps the pricks come out to play
It's Culture year so enter dear, raise your glass and make some din
But slam that door behind you... or those Scousers might come in.

Loved that by the way, so don't let no one tell you that *all* the
prickly people of this city have grabbed-a-hold of a rung on the
property ladder and disappeared into house-owning, money-chasing-
anonymity for good. Below that thin coat of Dulux there are thousands
of unheard souls just waiting to have a bit of dabble at this culture
thing – if given the chance.

Wintroduction

Nicky Allt

❧

n the year of 432 Saint Patrick sails down the River Mersey on his mission to Ireland. Go-ead Paddy la.

1207: King John signs a charter creating the borough of Liverpool and soon 800 people are sunbathing till a boat worth plundering goes by, or happy catching fish by the Mersey if there's not a heavy-laden schooner in sight.

1300s: First mayor whose name was Billy steps up and says 'Yeah, I've copped for the granny chain so I'm the Mayor.' From the first time he was seen wearing his mayoral chain, a circulated letter was passed around Ye old north west reporting that a thick gold chain had gone missing in Manchester. The headline: 'It was deffo a Scouser'.

1500s: Town hall built; then the first grammar school. Followed by the formation of the town council so lots of posh fellers became council-lors and immediately started in-fighting about where was the best place near the Pierhead to build a post for tying your horse to, where was the best place to part-ex a clapped-out horse, and who was the hardest pirate in Liverpool.

1600s: Liverpool became an independent port (can't we do that now?) and out of the taxing hands of the borough of Chester (now it's the borough of Westminster). And the first recorded cargo from America lands in Liverpool (part of it was strange tasting foodstuff from the New World – uncooked spuds – the first ever Unhappy Meal).

1700s: Population 5000, the first slave ship takes 220 slaves to Barbados. The first reference to Scouse gets recorded. The first circulating library in the world is built. Liverpool's Dr Dobson discovers the link between sugar and diabetes. Europe's first prison gets built (might've known). Liverpool's first newspaper (1712, *The Courant*) hits the streets. In effect the great-great-great-grandfather of the *Echo*. The first school for the blind built (it was built in the wrong place). First cargo of cotton gets traded (undies, socks and stringy-vests that doubled-up as fishing nets). The city becomes the only municipality with the right to issue its own money (again, can't we do that now with Ken Dodd on the twenties, Stan Boardman on the ten-spots and Mickey Finn on the blueys?). At the end of the century the town hall burns down as the posh fellers in-fight over who can light the best bommies.

1800s: Population 78,000. The first and only assassination of a British Prime Minister, Spencer Percival, shot by bankrupt Liverpool merchant John Bellingham. The first balloon ascent takes off from Liverpool and J. Sadler gets thrown from the balloon near Blackburn and dies. The first railway timetables, sheds and covered station are made in Liverpool, quickly followed by the first passenger fatality (William Huskisson). World's first school for deaf people gets built. The world's first transatlantic passenger service (to Boston) is opened by Cunard, and the world's first photograph developing and printing service starts up. The RSPCA is founded here. First girls' grammar school and world's first public baths opens. First shot in the American Civil War gets fired from a Liverpool-made gun. First rugby club, steamroller, cycling club, council houses, school of nursing, purpose-built library, medical officer (Dr Duncan) and slum clearance are up and out the blocks.

1800s cont... The last confederate ship to surrender (*Shenandoah*) does so at Liverpool Town Hall (rebels surrender at rebel town), and the first war disarmament campaign is started up by the Liverpool Peace Society (personally loved that fact – while men in their millions are being brainwashed into thinking it's fine to kill for Queen and Country, a bunch of rebellious Scouse hippies are the first to say 'No more war'). The first British public art gallery (Walker) and practising female doctor appear. The NSPCC gets founded, as do football nets (John Brodie), Everton FC (1878) and Britain's oldest mosque at Brougham Terrace. The Mersey Rail Tunnel (first underwater passenger tunnel in the world) and a host of docks are opened (Albert, Hornby, Canada, Langton, Wapping, Huskisson, Sandon, Wellington, Trafalgar, Victoria, Waterloo, Brunswick, Clarence, Canning, Princes), while the construction of St George's Hall is completed. Crawford's biscuits (1897) Princes foods (1880) and Tate and Lyle (1872) start up for business. In 1819 there was an Orange Order parade riot by the Billy Boys, but after the mass in-migration by hordes of starving Irish, before, during and after the Famine, the Fenians try to blow up the Town Hall. In 1892 Liverpool FC, England's most successful football team of all time, is formed.

1900s: Population 685,000; by 1937 it's 867,000. The largest tobacco warehouse in the world (27 million bricks) is built at Stanley Dock, and the brickies never once went on strike. The city's first tram and Britain's first fire engine and Woolworths store are on Liverpool's streets. The Liver Building clock starts ticking as revolution is in the air from the first major workers' strike. The police were given such a hard time during and after the 1911 dispute that by 1919 they became the first and only police force to ever go on strike. The first purpose-built boxing stadium and Mersey road tunnel open (Queensway 1934), as does the first two-way radio communication for British police.

1900s cont... Everton's Dixie Dean becomes the first footballer to hit 60 goals in a season, and Liverpool's Jack Balmer the first to score three consecutive hat-tricks. Liverpool songstress, Lita Roza, becomes the first female to hit the Number 1 spot ('How much is that doggy in the window?' 1953). The first police to use closed-circuit television and the first bank (Martins) and port (Mersey Docks and Harbour) to use computers are situated here in the city. The second Mersey tunnel opens (Kingsway 1971). The world's largest Anglican Cathedral has the biggest organ and heaviest peal of bells. (Ding dong, ding dong, our organ's this long.) The Catholic Cathedral (Paddy's Wig-Wam) opens for mass and communion in 1967, and the Pope eventually pays a visit in the 1980s as the Toxteth riots kick off and Liverpool police become the first to use tear gas on the rioters.

1900s cont... The Heysel (1985) and Hillsborough (1989) disasters hurt everybody deeply, none more so than the families involved. Meanwhile the English Football League title might as well be housed in Liverpool's Liver Building as the city's two teams virtually own it for the whole of the 1980s. All the while the people are to-ing and fro-ing, creating an individually stamped and dynamic type of culture all of their own (800 years in the making). The Beatles being the most

successful pop group of all time, and Liverpool the most successful
football team, in part allows the city to bid for, and win, the title of
European Capital of Culture 2008.

1900s cont... So here we are, finally in 2008, with me having a bash at
defining my hometown from the banks of our lovely Liverpool home.
The tales that follow are mine, alongside other Liverpudlian takes on
the culture of the city and culture year. Allied to these observations
are a few modern-day city stories, taking a glimpse into real Scouse
lives and how they go about their daily rituals on this their own manor.
Seeing as it's an un-English city – a mainly Celtic enclave – in a truly
Anglo-Saxon kingdom, I thought I'd start right there, at the point that
defines all things Scouse, and proudly makes it so.

Down at the Mersey seafront, breathing in that life-affirming, salty
air, I'm trying to hear the whispers of the millions of ghostly souls
that have disembarked here at this landing stage: our own Ellis Island.
Putting down roots here on English soil – like our forefathers did –
unquestionably makes us English. We carry the passport. But whoever
landed here also brought with them a volatile and fiery old affliction
called... the un-English disease. It's something we're all fortunate to
carry around with us to this day; something which gives us vitality
and keeps us edgy and different. If you're a born and bred Scouser or
you've lived here a while you'll know what I'm on about. If you don't
and you're just visiting, then I hope all you Culturites catch it... In fact,
let me rephrase that. Open your hearts, you might be lucky to catch
it!

The Un-English Disease

Nicky Allt

❧

Thing is, like I said, I only wanted to have a bash at defining my hometown, but believe me people of culture and people who want to know of our culture, that is a far from easy thing to do. See, I live in a city riddled with exceptions. You try to pin it down – to categorize it – and you're always going to come up like Tom Cruise does in real life. Recently walking with two mates through London before a football game, one of them turned to me and said, 'Look, there's that famous actor.' Looking over I thought he was on about Tattoo from Fantasy Island. Then I realized it couldn't be him unless he was wearing an Irish jig. Anyway, geographically in the North of England but definitely not of it, the surrounding villages, towns and cities have very similar economics, cultures and histories to each other but, undeniably, not to Liverpool.

Alongside the river and the sea it flows into, this apartness gives the Northern sailor town as close a shot at its true identity as you're going to get. If you're searching for a typical English city then Liverpool, again, is going to come up like Danny Devito without the heels. Where outsiders move in to eventually become insiders, and insiders move out but feel the need to retain strong ties with such an indelible place of birth, Liverpool, on an English city-scale, is the most changeable, volatile and unpredictable city on these shores. Scousers leave the city 'for the world' but it never leaves them. No wonder sailors of yester-year often bore the favoured tattoo of origin, 'made in Liverpool', etched around a sweaty salted bellybutton. If Tom Cruise had the same tattoo it could be viewed through an open-necked collar with ease. After seeing the actor in London it's probably easy to tell that I went home and watched a jarg DVD of *Mission Impossible 3* next day, because the famous Yankee midget's still jumping about in my skull!

As I tell you of my life in the city you must walk its streets with me and understand that these are the opinions of a Liverpool man who has lived his existence economically, culturally and historically within chiming distance of the nautical bells of St Nicholas's church by the old Pierhead. These are my estimations, and whether you agree or disagree I stand by them happily and unequivocally. I have had money, been skint; been happy as a Liver building seagull on a sunny July afternoon, and been drunk and disorderly and slept it off on stinking, old, Cheapside cell mattresses – but from my constant to-ings and fro-ings and climbs and falls, the word 'Liverpool' now sails through my arteries same as the electricity that surges down the wires every time you switch on your TV at night. I'm like a little stick of Liverpool rock... not as little as Tom Cruise... aaaghh forget him!

The politics of my father and his father, of my friends and neighbours, and of my living experience and upbringing may contrast sharply with yours and others, but still, they are my views and, like I said, if you're uncomfortable with them then you could go and read Tarby's, Cilla's or Cherie Blair's respective cultural biographies, or something similar for a more, shall we say... *professional* Liverpool take on things. I will try, as best I can, to tie down what being a Scouser and living in the city means today. But, even as we speak, monumental change and movement of people goes on all around, so this is an everyday tale of Liverpool life in 2008 as seen through my eyes.

For me, Liverpool is the Mersey, the Mersey is Liverpool. Whoa, give a big gold star to the Scottie Road rocket scientist who first came up with that esteemed observation. Yet it needed saying, as some people don't recognize just how sprinkled with salt from the Mersey we all are. As often happens on this information-overloaded planet a lot of truly educated people fail to see the wood for the trees – or the Mersey for the posh apartments these days – till somebody with a more simplistic view of life points out the glaringly obvious. I'll return to Scouse rocket scientists later... Our city grew on the edge of an Irish Sea inlet where shelter from its turbulent waters was often a necessity in earlier seafaring times. People told time by movement and swaying of the tides, not by the fingers of a Greenwich mean time clock. In the days when jumbo jets meant nothing more than a group of elephants taking a slash at London zoo, and travelling long distance meant week- to month-long epic sea voyages, Liverpool's docks and landing stages were busier than all the B&Q stores lumped together on a bank holiday Monday. And the great thing was, its shoreline swarmed with hard-nosed, seafaring students of life from every corner of the world; not the snot-nosed, part-time, retail park students, who don't know the difference between an air conditioner and a bottle of Wash and Go.

Sailors stopped here for a quick 'sustenance swallee', overstayed shore leave, and… er, stayed. While their ship set sail for the return journey to places like Sierra Leone, New York and Savannah, they had dropped anchor till further notice. Passengers did likewise. Often after feeling the fleetingly warm embrace of a local Mary Ellen, fleeting became meeting and those seas far too harsh to return to, as roots were put down on the banks of the rushing Mersey sound. Emigrants to the new worlds of the Americas and Australia, worried about returning to stormy waters after the first leg of a hazardous onward journey, often stayed put when their transportation docked at the Pierhead landing stage.

One of the first things emigrants noticed after disembarking at Liverpool's grand waterfront was the murky, brown colour of the sea; caused not by pollution or the thousands of Liverpool torpedoes yet to be flushed down the local drainage system, but by the rushing torrents that pushed their way up the Mersey estuary every day, lifting silt and sand from the bottom in the process. If the seabed which lay beneath the westerly waters of the Atlantic Ocean lapping at New York's waterfront was supposedly laden with the bodies of mob hits and gangland war victims, à la Tony Soprano, then Liverpool's seabed was laden with the ashes of a thousand souls happy to be laid to rest there after they'd died from far more natural causes. Always a city with more sarky pranksters than narky gangsters, legend has it that if you are down at the old Pierhead at the dead of night and you listen long and hard enough you can hear the laughing of Liverpool's dearly departed, eternally happy to be laid to rest in the river they so loved in life.

When my Liverpool life is done and it's time to bury me
Take me down to the old Pierhead and throw me in the sea
No ship-like coffin in the ground was ever meant for me
Cos my salt-sprayed River Mersey is were I'll spend eternity

Jimmy Fagan… old Liverpool sailor

As Liverpool bay sucks in the swelling waters of the passing Irish Sea then its city sucks in people from all over the world who were only supposed to tickle its shores before embarking for the next destination. Liverpool can do that to people. Feeling the warmth of its embrace, the humour of its people and wearing the dancing shoes of its streets, often for one passing weekend only, has, on thousands of occasions, turned into a lifetime lodging where family trees were long-term seeded and planted. Ship's captains and their owners often dreaded the Liverpool port of call as half the crew wouldn't return from shore-leave, leaving them moored-up till new deck-handed sailor-boys were found. And even if you told time by the movement of the sea, sea time was still money to the ship-owning paymasters of the day.

An original sin city, Russian, German and Norwegian captains were often first to jump ship. Scabby-arsed, scurvy-ridden ship with a scabby-arsed, flea-riddled crew made urchin-freckled embrace all the more alluring and all the harder to leave behind. It's the old *Letter to Brezhnev* syndrome where Russian sailor meets local girl and ship's leave ends up in an inter-continental weave of Haircut 100 singing 'Boy meets Girl'... a bit like the famous 'Leaving of Liverpool' folk song. And that, my friend, is the sweet version of people stopping here. The other more numerous and less romantic take is the one where, with no food and money, destitute and broke, they couldn't face the second leg of an onward journey to the faraway New World and upped and jibbed ship. Once sailor-boy was entrenched in Liverpool's water-front party streets by day and early evening, and dossing down under Mary Ellen's ragged shawl by night, a short stop for a few drams on dry land frequently turned into a lifetime mooring.

Check the city phone book, or the deaths and births pages of local newspapers, there alongside your Smiths and Stevensons you'll find an abundance of names from every corner of the world. Plenty of Irish Fagans, Farrells and Flahertys; a profusion of Italian Baccinos, Tremarcos and Ventres; a gathering of Wongs, Changs and Sangs; a whole host of African Gibilrus, Ackinwandes and Contehs; not forget-ting the thousands of Celtic Welsh Bennetts, Williams and Edwards, and a proud proliferation of Scottish Celt Macs. Oh, and lest we forget, they once battled for a Water or Dale Street basement lodging along-side those same Norwegian, German and Russian sailors who had also jumped ship through lack of cash, want of work, or due to the warm, loving embrace of dock-dubber Mary Ellen.

This colourful array of ocean transients all decided to settle here upon the banks of the most un-English city in England. At the head of many a family tree the great grandfather will usually attest to the truth in the old Liverbirds adage that, 'If y'standin' on a corner, all alone an' feelin' low, a Liverbird will come an' get yer, singin' Eee

Aye Addio'. Mythology – maybe – but more than a grain of truth in Michael McCartney's melody nobody can deny.

Emigrants to New York, sailing up the Hudson River before stepping onto land near the checking gates of Ellis Island, had certainly arrived. Most emigrants sailing up the Mersey before hitting dry ground prior to docking in Liverpool would be thinking 'How long will I stop here?', being more frequently bound for somewhere else. Under the microscope of the heavens the heaving dock front was a sand block stepping-stone forever being lapped at and lashed at by gushing brown water, all the while teeming with a rag-taggle, brim-full-of-life.

The stipendiary magistrate's records of 1847 told of 296,000 Irish landing at these shores in one year alone; a cold, stiff-upper-lipped English landlord, a failed potato crop and 'the Famine' starving them away from their infertile mother country. Most were identifiable as instant paupers, vagrants and thieves, landing in Liverpool with no possessions, malnourished to the bone and wearing nothing but the rags they shuffled down the splintered gangplank in. With ship sores, scabs and heartbreak being the only form of baggage, first foot bathe in the Mersey meant the salty river became the disinfectant Dettol of the day.

With New York being the gateway to the land of so-called opportunity those same poor huddled masses arrived at its doorstep with total destination in mind. Arriving in Liverpool, bedraggled and starving, they were at port terminus to catch the next big ship to the New World. A daunting prospect when you'd spent long starving days on the nautical roller-coaster called the Irish Sea. Eventually landing at Liverpool docks you could be on the lookout for a ship to any corner of the world; if you landed by rail at Lime Street Station you were already at destination. An early Liverpool saying went, 'Making a stand, travel by land. Where do you want to be? Travel by sea.'

The fact that most who filed through the port were destitute meant thousands never took that onward passage, remaining strapped-trapped in Liverpool's warren of streets and jiggers, wandering them in search of food, a job and respite. Meanwhile, the city's resources were overwhelmingly stretched to the limit. Being able to laugh in the face of adversity is a characteristic those people have undoubtedly passed down through the years to today's occupants. Though as times change and we become more and more materially dependent (Americanized), it seems the majority of the population would be more likely to pray for divine intervention if they were made to go without their TV remotes, car keys or mobile phones for a day than fresh air or health itself. Uneducated and predominantly from rural villages, many of those starving Irish thought they were already in New York. It's one of the reasons why New York's population grew dramatically over decades, and Liverpool's instantly, yet less so over years – still measurably, but not on the grand or long-term scale of New York. Who knows where the city would be now if we'd had Hollywood movies and the selling technique of the Yanks.

The fact that Liverpool's numbers exploded over a short period of time – during and after the Irish potato famine – is testament to its standing as the main port city of the Great British Empire around the middle of the nineteenth century. In its Victorian heyday it became a hubbub for business, culture and civilization by the sea, and while its numbers grew rapidly from long-distance (across the sea) in-migration, its neighbouring settlements – Blackburn, Bolton and Manchester – grew from the joining together of small towns, helped along by short-distance in-migration (across land) from the surrounding rural areas (allied to the Welsh influx, it's why everyone talked with a farm-like Maaa till we began to speak with a shanty-type Laaa). As an example of your average Northern English settlement and how small towns knitted themselves together to form a city, see Manchester. For Liverpool, or, for New York, as John Lennon once said, see Liverpool times ten. Today, make that fifteen or twenty times, as New York's population scale goes way off the proliferation radar, while Liverpool's tapered off some years ago. With the sea as a natural wall boundary, so Liverpool grew naturally as a city along its waterfront.

From normal sea shanty beginnings, where licensed pirates had flourished year after year (the original scallies with small skull and crossbones badges instead of the tiny crocodile), Liverpool as a city only started to explode once rich merchants began to use its natural seafront to deal in slaves, slavery and other ill-gotten gains from foreign lands around the globe. See, people are often brainwashed into thinking that we need investment from the corporate company men, but those scally pirates had a tremendously profitable graft up and on the go long before Mr Moneyman arrived in town with his slavery and keenness to make a packet. He may have put Liverpool on the map but the greedy need for begging-bowl casual labour meant he never attempted to take the poor off of it.

Like hip-hop, like clubs, like fashions and trends, it more often than not begins on the streets, or in this case, on and along the river, till some be-suited bread-head has to come along and re-package and box it off for profit and ultimate mega-wealth. And fact is, throughout the city's growth and wealth surge the contrast between rich and poor remained greater than in almost any city in the world. Rich merchants began to line well-stitched pockets and build gloriously fantastic structures and monuments to capitalism, while unemployment, drunkenness and crime in Liverpool were still the worst in Britain. Entrepreneurs who came to make their fortune after hearing of this new bustling cosmopolitan city by the sea were instantly astounded when greeted by modern buildings of beauty and stature, but, checking behind their façades, equally astonished at the contrasting dungeons of squalor that lay at the foot of some of the most marvellous structures in the Western world.

Liverpool's bay was an ideal harbouring shelter for stockpiling in-coming and out-going goods and sea vessels, and carpet-bagging merchants were quick to seize the money-making initiative by setting up home and business along its shoreline. The English government, deciding likewise, built the first modern dock in the world, to have its navy frigates at the ready. Its closeness to Ireland and the Englishmen's need to dominate and exploit that country's land, people and resources was a main reason, if not *the* major reason, for maritime construction. Next came warehouses, churches and theatres as Liverpool became nineteenth-century civilized on new-found wealth. Canals were sliced and thousands of small boats made their way in. Docks were built and huge ships and liners brought goods and people from all around the world. Lighthouses were erected and began to twinkle nightly along the River Mersey. Posh balls and newspapers were introduced for Liverpool gentlemen and women (one man's printed piece of paper became the *Echo* and one woman's all-dancing gin house eventually became Cream) as the city surged past London and Bristol for sea trade on an entrepreneurial wave of commercial aggression.

By 1850, one third of Britain's commerce was Liverpool inspired. With the first railway built by George Stephenson (the city was racking up more firsts than its football teams and the Beatles put together) and a canal system carving its way into the industrial heartlands of West Yorkshire and the Midlands, the visiting American consul called it 'the greatest commercial city in the world'. Kings and queens, princes and princesses, dukes, emperors and shahs from all corners of the globe wanted to pay homage and visit the port that did double the trade of London, half that of the whole nation and more overseas and foreign trade than any other place on the planet.

With the Mersey suffering from vessel congestion and hulls laden with expensive goods and finery from all corners, those long-gone pirates could have done with hanging around New Brighton and Formby Point till the mid-nineteenth-century boom. But maybe they'd found more honest employment as glorious buildings were constructed on the strength of the port controlling the world market for cotton and grain, and being the world leader in soap, sugar and salt manufacture and in all insurance interests. If the sons of those pirates had kept one eye patched on plunder and robbery on the high seas, while gaining employment as insurance clerks and bosses, they could've beaten the New York Mafia to the old con of stealing everything a business has to offer, before claiming the double-earner of an insurance payout shortly after (see Long Firm con).

The city's population paid the highest property and income taxes outside London, but I can assure you nobody who voted and could afford to pay complained, because they definitely saw more for their gilded guinea than the use of a purple bin and an indoors-only Mathew Street festival. Not only were the powers that be spending their money on link roads, canals and magnificent architecture, they were also planning and landscaping more parks than any other provincial city on the atlas; all the while trying to offset the congested seaport area like they were on a 'fresh air for the people mission'.

As always their money never tinkled down to the mass underclass, and the poverty-stricken grew in numbers as wealth and opulence increased for the few. Divide and conquer remained order of the day, with people having to clamber over each other for work because of a casual labour system put in place by Liverpool's landed gentry. Though they'd have been better putting an end to casual labour by opening businesses with more solid 'long-term' employment, Liverpool's movers and shakers were still far-sighted as leaders on the world stage, and face it, it's always easier with more charitable, historical hindsight.

Anyway it needs saying here and now, 'Oh where art thou, far-sighted Liverpool leaders of yesteryear?', men who could not only see way further than the end of their well-powdered noses (not the mind-numbing cocaine of today, but from forever dipping their noses into the life-affirming Mersey, sniffing for ever more opportunity) but were also visionary in viewing the city as a world leader and player in all games of commerce available. Whereas they thought of rivalling other great ports in trade and commerce, and other great cities for beauty of buildings and infrastructure, now they have costly debates lasting a year about whether or not they should build a museum, while all the while thinking what might be in it for them and their local ladder-climbing careers.

Always there in the background, in stark contrast to Liverpool's pomp, hidden away behind brand-new structures of marvel, lay dirty narrow lanes where people read Bibles in twenty different languages and drank and fought in the streets to a standstill as the stinking little gin houses multiplied. As trumpets of civilization and wealth were sounded a ratio of one gin house to every forty people became an unwanted statistic and the social conditions of the poor still remained the poorest imaginable. Through it all the street-hardened, steely-eyed, bundle of vitality that was Mary Ellen strode on in times of hardship to eventually settle this city's bedrock population. Its musical, sporting and cultural prowess all began in Mary's sturdy loins.

In the bedding and telling of Liverpool history and folklore it is usually the men who are spoken of when dishing out praise, distaste or notoriety concerning the making, breaking or shaking of the city, but when it comes to pure 'in yer face' Liverpool DNA it's the women who have helped bend and shape 'yer average Scouser' more than anyone. Take a walk through Liverpool's main carnival streets and behold their striking beauty, their loud, throaty, roaring laugh and their ferocious appetite to party. There you will witness the gyrating loins and birth-place of true Liverpool DNA (ignore the Penny Farthing and Blob boozers of today, where you will more likely find the birthplace of the female gummy midget).

I have travelled the world extensively and, without wishing to sound like the Warren Beatty of Bootle, on occasion had the company of females from most parts of the globe, and (this is an opinion I share with the vast majority I have spoken to) never have I come across in such numbers ladies with a passion to laugh, live and love like the Liverpool ladies. Good God dear boy, do those good-time girls know how to party! Like the tatty-headed one with the Queen Anne legs once sang, 'You're simply the best' and here, to them, I duly raise a toast. (It's a pint of Beck's at the Casa on Hope Street where I'm now writing this, and seeing as it's Friday afternoon and I'm in a Brendan Behan of a mood I think I'm allowed a quick three…) The Liverpool prosti-tutes who beckoned the first stepping-stoners off the boat (Maggie May, Titch Maguire, Cast Iron Kitty, Jumping Jenny, and hundreds of Mary Ellens being among the famous names) were said to have been under more sailors than a Titanic toilet. Considering Maggie May's toughness to survive in harsh, trying conditions, it's a definite truth considering how long the beautiful big ship lasted.

While the city grew wealthy and its name spread far and wide, news of a prosperous place on the north-west coast of England eventually reached the poor of Europe and Ireland. The sailors of other countries had already sent message back of this 'bouncing city by the sea'; now their even poorer, land-bound-lubber relations began to set sail in their hordes. The port area became chaotic with more than a thousand houses of prostitution open for 'off the ship and in for a dip' business, as Mary Ellen first sought a wage and a good time. Always the best at finding a good time and with incoming business and new Mary Ellens arriving daily, she couldn't afford to fall ill or take a day off. Portside doctors of the day were famous for examining then dishing out the same advice to any sickly Mary Ellen: 'Try staying out of bed for a week'. It was said these girls of the curls and twirls were so prevalent around the dockland area that they outnumbered the streetlamps that were also similarly *turned on at night on every street corner*. Mary's Mary was working harder than a Garston tugboat with the QE2 in tow.

Show a Liverpool girl a good time and she'll give you her heart and soul. I know, because during my travels when Liverpool was becoming a bit too much – it happens now and again, especially when Liverpool seems small and the built-in wanderlust kicks in – I often thought about settling down in far sunnier and salubrious climes, only to come legging it home when the throaty roar of Liverpool and its ladies grew far too strong to resist. The constant need to trek, eh… it's in the blood, what can you do? But often, more so when down at the Mersey seafront and looking out to sea, the need to set sail, to travel and to escape one's confines grows too hard to resist, and the urge for travel can sometimes become overwhelming. Liverpool girls and the humour allied to the intoxicating smell of the Mersey were always a heady mix to bring you right back down to earth once again though. I would go as far as to say that these three things mixed together were the early drunken sailors' Viagra and a massive shot in the arm for Liverpool's growing population. It seemed at times that every time Sailor Joe arrived back in Liverpool a new pregnancy was announced. Families the size of football teams with three or four substitutes became the norm.

Look, concerning the mating game: if you are a man who struggles to make conversation with the opposite sex then I advise you to migrate to the city centre like those sailors of old – dressed clean and smart of course – and there they will talk to you and save you the bother. Engage them decently, buy them a bevvy, and you won't get a word in edgeways. Take note: you must show some warmth and facial expression – happy or sad. If you're sad they'll want to know who upset you and want to make you smile. If you're already smiling and laughing they'll want to know what all the joviality is about and what they're missing out on. No facial expression, with a John Major, all-round paving-flag grey about you – forget it! Saying that, even Liverpool girl Edwina Currie eventually found a lighthouse twinkling in ol' John's grey eye, a place I think many other females on these shores might have found a struggle to get a twinkle going.

The following is titled:

Prison Ship Postcard

Mary Ellen how I think of you
When far from shore and Liverpool
Bound for Boston weeks for sure
I'll soon be waged and at your door

While this Yankee Clipper bends and creaks
And through its racket your soft voice speaks
It'll come whispering to me on Atlantic air
And that's where I find my comfort there

But soon we'll dock then I'll be bound
To the place I love with familiar sounds
Where I'll spend my coin and make my hay
To stop for good with you someday

Oh urchin freckles of hardened stock
Of tattered shawl and lacey frock
Come meet my ship and comfort me
This time I'll not return to sea

Whether it be passing sailors or boring John Majors those Mary Ellens of the Mersey are the main reason why Scouse DNA captured the title of the Capital of Culture for 2008. She either gave birth to the entrepreneurs, personalities and workers who built and moulded the most successful businesses in Liverpool, or coddled, fed and helped nurture the most identifiable characteristics in this city; the humanity of the people, the football teams, Littlewoods, Vernon's, Matalan, the musicians (Beatles, Bunnymen, Merseybeat etc. etc.), Cunard, White Star, Tate, Scouse lingo and its tough veneer, dockers, sailors, writers, comedians, I could go on and on and on. Often the men were away at sea, or working long hours on the docks or in lowly paid jobs. Even the entrepreneurs had to have strong women who supported them as they built business empires. All the while Liverpool's women were there, sturdy and proud, holding the fort together. And face it: it was Scouse DNA that got the ties and suits clamouring to bestow the city with the inventively created award. Another thing: are we bothered as Liverpool people as a whole? I think we were, till we realized it was for the benefit of those same shirts and ties to pat themselves on the back, take all the good jobs that came riding on in and spend all the culture money on events and happenings that nobody gave a flying fart about.

Personally, I couldn't give a sailor from Sierra Leone's shite about 'their award', but I suppose it's par for the course for stuffed shirts to tell you you have won an award for your culture, then totally ignore your culture when the funding for events gets sorted. Don't get me wrong, like most Liverpudlians I'll still raise a glass, but, for me, it's like a British Rail gravy train to the Northern city of 'Yer havin'a'laugh' that ended up mobbed with ladder-climbing, pinstriped goons all waiting to vulture themselves into a hot seat on the new Culture Board. I can almost hear them as the award was won: 'Where's next for graft Smithers old boy?' 'Obviously the Capital of Culture don't you think?' The embarrassing thing for me and other Liverpudlians is not that they fail to do their job before running off with wedge once all's done 'n' dusted, it's the fact that the hierarchy in Liverpool hire them in the first place. It's like they're thinking these serial job surfers are going to give the city an edge we don't already possess, or bring something different to a party and culture that's been eight hundred years in the making. It's seriously embarrassing – FACT!

Listen, outside influence and centralization of power to London has bled the North, and Liverpool in particular, of resources and natural-born leaders for long enough. What do we get in their place? Handouts and fancy-titled executives coming up to take the best jobs with no ambition to stay and fight for the good of the city, and with no willingness to put down any type of family roots like the far-sighted forefathers of yesteryear. Their contribution to Liverpool life is forever glorified at the outset, and nearly always found to be wanting and superficial at termination. Too often great Liverpool-born ideas are frustrated or put on the shelf by outsider officialdom, outsider finance houses or London boardroom decisions.

If we want to be a truly thriving, successful city – again – we need to look within our own hearts and within our own boundary walls. They say that Scousers are often too insular and the out-of-town woollyback view is that we are big-headed. I say to that: we should be more insular in looking for leaders, ideas and ways to make our city truly great again. Executive job surfers are like mercenary footballers who make all the right noises early on and start kissing the badge after two minutes, but soon as things get tough or they're not in the limelight, or the team, its offski to the the next big payday. The big-headed thing out-of-towners accuse us of is often born of jealousy, as Liverpool is full of dreamers of grand designs. Well, without the dream, nothing happens. So I say to that: no more apathy, dream more, dream bigger and drag yourself up by your bootstraps and make those dreams reality. In other words think for yourself and be bigger-headed!

Liverpool is obviously 'different' from other English cities. You need to live here for at least a few years to fully understand that truth. Yet the local powers that be hand out jobs to passing pinstriped ships, who would not only struggle to find their way to the Mersey while not having a clue about the city's history, its make-up or the DNA of its people, but were never intending to stay or settle here for any length of time in the first place. I mean, what's wrong with employing a rock solid Royal Iris who has known these waters and sailed these shores for a number of years? You learn to appreciate a bowl of Scouse (with red cabbage) over a period of time, digested slowly. Eaten quickly over a short space of time, it might as well be stroganoff or goulash.

It seems to the man in the street like a case of 'jobs for the boys', or they're giving their old academic mates a bunk-up while simultaneously taking the piss out of the local populace – big time! It's as though they presume the locals are not up to the jobs on offer, you know, seeing as we didn't get the recognized degree or diploma in how to organize our own cultural celebrations. Ha! Look, as a young kid I remember Bruce Forsyth (a compere with a degree in compering) trying to conduct the Liverpool supporters to sing on cue before the 1974 FA Cup Final. They ignored and mocked him to such an extent that frustrated and bemused he trudged from the Wembley turf after totally giving up. Listen to the singing of the national anthem every time Liverpool or

Everton are in the FA Cup Final and you will not only find a reluctance
to sing the outdated 'God Save the Queen' ditty; among the whistles
and taunts you will also find the only crowd in Britain who will rebel
against singing just for the sake of it, or because they're being told
where and when they should and shouldn't. Bringing people in to tell
Liverpool people how to party? It's like selling snow to the Eskimos;
an absolute piss-take in the extreme!

And while I'm on, no disrespect an' all that but I've just heard
Ringo's the top drawer entertainment the 'men in the know' have
lined up. Wow! Now there's a Californian Scouser to get the party
going: Zimmer frame made from old drumsticks, map to Dingle and
a three-hour rehearsal about 'what city are we in tonight maaan?' Bet
it took a trademark Ringo peace-sign, a couple of hundred grand and
all of two-and-a-half minutes to work that one out! Ringo might be a
good lad an' all that, but, face it, Lily Savage with a tightly-strapped
Birkenhead ball-bag and a voice like a fork on a plate is more of a
Scouser than Ringo these days. Now Macca of the Beatles I could've
understood. One seriously talented man who has always had his head
screwed on, except for one recent lapse – and we're all allowed one of
those – when he married 'some bird' a few years ago?

And, jokes apart, get this; maybe Ringo only got the St Georges
Hall gig now that he's got a mid-Atlantic accent? Y'know, now he's lost
the heavier Dingle part of it somewhere over the Bermuda Triangle,
because sometimes… er, maybe we all talk 'too Scouse' – seriously!
Being an un-English accent what can you do? Want to be a big noise at
the party or get a top job on the Culture Board, or in some other higher
sphere of Liverpool working life? – lose the accent, or smother it in
soft as a pillow, marshmallow English. Saying that, I met the Liverpool
Labour leader Joe Anderson in the theatre the other night and Joe was
as Scouse as they come, so hopefully things are changing. Put the accent
thing this way: if there was a top job interview taking place in England
for a vacancy at NASA to teach astronauts the right and wrong way to
land on the moon and the world's joint-leading rocket scientist spoke
with a heavy Brummie accent, nobody would believe him. Try it, you'll
see what I mean. If the world's other leading rocket scientist spoke with
a strong Scouse accent, first they'd search him for his certificates then
they'd tell him they'd given the job to the Brummie.

It often seems like we can't employ our own because they're too
harsh of speech, too guttural and too regional… er, in other words too
Liverpudlian? Like we're too timid to believe in ourselves, our own

and our own voice, and only an outsider with a different accent can 'know the score'. Concerning out-of-town and people's perceptions of Scousers, although I don't agree, I can understand why a Scouser wouldn't get the NASA job, but when it comes to Liverpool jobs... bah! It's just not on! It's like, say you need a 30-to-40-grand-a-year local radio presenter, you want the person to know all about Liverpool music and what the listeners want, you go and ask Billy Butler. Ten out of ten assumption and well in by the way for using simple under-your-nose logic. Now, next, for at least a hundred grand a year, and up, you want someone to run the Culture Company and its celebrations, you go and get a full-on 100 per cent 'in the know' Liverpool person, yeah, you'd think so... Well, no, what we'll do is we'll go and bring in Jason Harborow from culturally aware Chorley and Robyn Archer (she fired an arrow and hit the jackpot called Liverpool) from er... marvellous bleeding Melbourne, Australia... they're bound to know the score, especially concerning all things Liverpool.

This one's the ten out of ten ultimate, piss-taking, follow-through-fart-of-a-joke! And, sadly and apathetically, we still put up with it. Oh yeah, we have a bit of a moan now and again, while sitting in armchairs reading about *their* next financial cock-up in the *Echo* pages. But we really need to step up and into the face of the ones who employ these people in the first place (if we can find them). As Liverpool people, and as before, we need to take matters into our own hands, otherwise things in this city will never change or move along and, like I've already said, change and movement is what gave us this culture and what we were always about. Moaning at a newspaper report from an armchair viewpoint never changed a fucking lightbulb!

Because of past local tendency to be in-your-face, nonconformist and razor sharp at cutting through the bullshit, maybe, just maybe, a local Scouser might get the job done, and make the usual suits look like they once again looked when handling funding for the 2007 Mathew Street festival and the Culture Company itself: like the inept bull-shitters they are and always have been. Twenty million pound shortfall and the cap-in-hand goes out to central government once again? And we as so-called mouthy Scousers let it happen, year after year; because it's nothing new this Billy Bullshit game, is it? Will it change? WILL IT FUCK! Not while we're all too busy paying our own mortgages and having a sly moan from our armchairs whenever we feel the need. Apathy, eh... and all the while local councillors in-fight and waste precious time making things easy for the divide and conquer brigade down in South East Tory Central. Short-sightedness by councillors and the apathy of the populace: the biggest diseases to strike at the well-meaning man on the Liverpool street. Big headedness (dreaming big), far-sightedness (seeing the bigger picture) allied to getting up off your arse and in-the-face: forever the way forward for Liverpudlians to change things for the better. Once and for all!

Look, part of what I'm saying about the accent is: people are mobile today, the world's a smaller place, but go job-hunting to Wigan, Manchester or most of surrounding lambswool Lancashire (woollyback-land) with that same Scouse accent in tow and you've already got an A1 chance of pulling the interview short straw just on speech alone – it's tough being a Scouser at times. Ha ha! Yeah, still we laugh. Me, I love the challenge... well, sort of love it because it can be annoying at times, because face it... it's true. Though often, it must be said, it makes me giggle at the ridiculousness of it all. But when we can't get the local jobs, especially the top local jobs, then it's like some sort of employment double-whammy! As a byword, those institutions of business surrounding the city boundaries should take note and employ Liverpool girls only. Not only would they brighten the workplace up with some throaty laughter and a little Liverbird intuition, they might help colour the cheeks and lives of many a shady-grey, office dude.

The prejudices that Liverpool people face in the UK quickly evaporate once leaving these shores. Being a Scouser and a Liverpool person can often mean being held in reverence in other countries. I have been treated well and held in esteem by Australians, Americans and South Africans just because of where I come from, yet been treated with heavy-handedness and intolerance by people I share a passport and a nationality with. It's usually the accent that sees to that. You state it clearly, when it's happening, and all you get back is the whingeing Scouser theory – as I'm probably getting right now from the unenlightened. Am I looking for sympathy? You can shove your sympathy up the old trap two. Am I looking for opportunity and equality? Too fucking right I am! If you're a local Liverpudlian and you've never noticed it then maybe you don't travel around the UK much, but I can assure you those that do will attest to what I'm saying in far greater numbers.

Who knows, maybe it's a case of familiarity (on TV, down the road, Scouse enclaves) breeds contempt? I remember once standing in a bank queue in Bournemouth waiting my turn, till the teller, and then manager, made me wait while several checks were undertaken to prove my identity and that the 3000 pounds (redundancy money) invested were indeed mine. After twenty minutes, and only when I was allowed the use of the bank's phone and put through to a Castle Street, Liverpool, branch manager, were the Bournemouth staff told in no uncertain terms that I was a valued customer and should be served immediately. Nobody else queuing for weekend spends in that long Friday afternoon queue was asked for ID, or told to wait by the wall like a disobedient school kid. The customers and staff stared on as a commotion was made by a short-sighted, clueless suit of a manager who had spoken to me like I was John Dillinger on a southern coast rampage. Leaving the building he told me that Scousers were the reason for 'ALL' the crime in his hometown, and that crime statistics were almost zero per cent till the Scousers started arriving in town in the late 70s and early 80s. He had me thinking that local prisons like Dorchester must have been built for pension and life-savings racketeers with all the wrinklies, like him, that crowded Bournemouth's streets.

This was not an isolated incident, or a persecution complex in overdrive. I know this has happened to thousands of other Liverpool people while at work or holidaying around the UK. At the time (mid-80s) the same southern seaside resort had the temerity to announce that only five Scousers were allowed in each Sunday League football team – seriously – due to the Liverpool lads who'd gone to work there during the Milk Snatcher years organizing their own football teams and quickly winning the local leagues and cups with ease. Imagine if that ruling had been made concerning black, Asian or Polish footballers? My mates John Burke from Scotland Road and Kevin Rowan from pop group Our Kid lived there for years and used to laugh about how they were viewed. A lot of those young Scousers went out of their way to annoy the narrow-minded, well-to-do, older populace by trying to bed as many of their beautiful, young daughters as possible – pre-AIDS days these. John eventually stood as a Labour councillor just for a wind-up and a laugh, and though Hannibal Lecter would've gotten more votes, it achieved what it was supposed to by getting right up local wrinkly noses.

Closer to home and more recently, while attending a school re-union dinner, a policeman who trained other police officers in Lancashire – being the best at his job – told me how any Scouser stopped in the Lancashire region was instantly under suspicion and that nearly all non-Liverpool officers he worked with held bigoted views connecting Liverpool people with crime. I could write a book full of tales about Scouser-phobia but being a male I wonder if this is a man-only thing and if any Liverpool ladies have ever suffered the same disrespect around the UK? Who knows? Maybe their charm and beauty gets them the instant respect that a Liverpool man would never get (bedraggled crackhead whores apart).

From the pyjama-wearing scallywagesses to the newly created moneywags, many men on foreign shores, from truly loaded pop stars to teenage Magaluf monkeys, have felt the intoxicating whiff and enjoyed grabbing onto the love handles of the new out 'n' about 'Scouse bird'. A secret delicacy for years, kept hidden away from the rest of the country by overly protective and often downright jealous young Liverpool men, who wanted Mary Ellen and Maggie May – especially on payday – all to themselves, the scallywagesses and moneywags have their own money and their own wheels today. So there you have it, time stands still for no one and the rest of Britain is finally waking up to the fact that we have the finest ladies on the island bar none.

Yeah, for Capital of Culture read Scouse bird DNA. And I don't mean that in a derogatory sense. When I say bird, though it was always local slang for the female part of the boyfriend–girlfriend relationship, it always reminded me of that that big metal Liverbird stood atop of the Liver buildings, the female Mother of all Liverpool. There you have it: Scouse bird DNA. Try introducing it into the Royal Family and we'd see a marked difference in chin-shape, musical flair and sporting prowess in all of nine months. If anyone dropped the first Scouse egg and it cracked, which, in truth, made us all crackers, it was that big metal lady standing there chest out in all weather, chewing away nonchalantly in a gale-force wind for fun. For a fine three-minute take on the more flesh-like of what I'm saying try listening to Ian McNabb's aptly titled song 'Liverpool Girl' from his *Merseybeast* album, or even the old traditional Irish lament of 'Liverpool Lou', best sung by the fantastic Dubliners… as I have it.

While conforming has never been a Liverpudlian strong point (un-Englishness) the fact we always had so many nonconformists meant the place often seemed edgy, and was always rich in character and with characters because of that edginess. And so were born a hundred and one TV and stage stars – once given the green light to perform, that is. 'People performing' is a daily street ritual of Liverpool life, and if the TV cameras were only willing to leave London a little more we might see the second wave or newer version of Merseybeat upon our screens and front pages sooner rather than later. And believe me, with an appetite to entertain that cannot be quelled by dribs and drabs and the odd handout from London-centric arts-and-media movers and shakers it will definitely explode again one day. This I feel in my bones. This I know.

Face it: the place is teeming with talent, and once a little River Mersey water seeps through, and it will, it could mean the onset of the collapsing of the dam that was built somewhere just north of Watford Gap in the early seventies. I'm 90 per cent on this. Bear with me as I explain. My 10 per cent doubt is that as the seeds of Scouseness get over-watered with possessions and comfort, I often wonder if the psyche of people performing will get drowned out by sameness and 'everywhere else' type wealth. You get an elegantly built home with all the smothering upgrades and a fridge full of top scoff, you don't want to leave it at six o'clock on a January morning to cut a disc at a freezing-cold recording studio because it's the only slot available to record the new song you co-wrote, and that you might only sell a hundred copies of (McCartney, McManus and McNabb). You don't want to leave the internet and a warm velour seat to drive fifteen miles to night school in mid-November to learn script writing and hopefully, hopefully put yourself in the frame as the next great TV or play writer (Bleasdale, Russell and McGovern). You don't want to go to acting school same night, 'ah there's thousands out there already' (Morrissey, Hart and Schofield), or go out to the garden shed to paint that picture that you've always wanted to show to people, and so release your real hidden talent for art (Tony Brown of 100 heads fame, Arthur Dooley of Jesus sculpture and Adrian Henri of poetry and art).

See, it's all this new-found wealth that takes the edginess out of an edgy city, not hard times. Whereas at my age I still feel a need to rebel against government and political wrong-doing, maybe the younger generation don't feel that need – that knot in the stomach – and have somehow forgotten how to rebel – or they need a remote control button before they'll have a bash. In a place where art and expression were always a huge part of daily life – an escape – where men had to find work abroad, or on ships a long, long way from home comforts and loved ones, and life was lived and loved and told through those eyes, I wonder where the new driven artists and storytellers will emerge from? The talent is there. It's embedded in their DNA. The wrongs to be righted are there (war, starving countries, chemicals in our food). But will they all drown in an ocean of material possessions and debt and let their true talent be blunted and sanded down by the comforts of modern life? I see younger, but I don't see hunger. And that is my only worry for the next generation of new kids on this still edgy, but no doubt less edgy, block.

Comforts of the Western world can drown the soul: the phones, computers, flash houses, cars and bank accounts. Experiencing life, travel, being with family and friends and in solitude – in equal amounts – and being both rich and poor in equal measure; these are things that make and nourish a creative soul. To live in a city full of edgy souls is a wondrous thing for creativity. I strive to be creative. To drown that inventive DNA in a sea of pot-bellied comforts, isolated internet living and wealth is a frightening thought indeed. On occasion I have heard so-called educated outsiders refer to Scouse humour as childlike or childish because of its generally insular, scathing and sardonic nature. If a child in infant years is the purest reflection of the soul, unwarped and untouched, then long may Liverpool people remain childlike. Whenever I travel far from home for any length of time it's Liverpool humour I miss above anything.

By the way, we're not the only city in the world with its finger on the chuckle-button, but it's no coincidence that other port cities have people of similar caustic humour (New York and Marseille for example). It's a thing to be cherished and held in worth, like you do when you are away from it for any length of time. Believe me when I say today's mad dash for money, possessions and wealth is totally against the flow of nature – and fun. And face it, unlike the seriously harsh times our forefathers were used to after jumping ship at the old Pierhead, or even as recently as the early eighties, locally life is not really as hard as it was, life is really *too* easy comparatively. Too easy isn't enriching or good for the soul, yet the race for more comforts and more riches pushes on seemingly unabated. Unlike the politicians and 'bottom-jaw like a till-drawer' moneymen, I'm all for shouting 'hold yer horses concerning Liverpool Tonto, and once again, shove your major corporate up the old trap two!'

A somewhat sketchy version of the Liverpool identity is known all over the UK and, in some sense, the world. From Tony Booth's lovable rogue in *Till Death Us Do Part*, to the Randall and Hopkirk ghost, to Rigsby, Yozzer, Scully, Corkhill, Rita, Jim Royle, Enfield's Scousers, Boswells, Beatles, Pacemakers, Cilla and a hundred and one more Freddie Starrs of the TV stage, it seems everyone has an idea or take on what the make-up of a Liverpudlian is all about. It's about as strong an opinion on a city identity as you're likely to get, especially here in the UK. At times I think this grates on other less talented cities, and so

Liverpool is up on some sort of talent pedestal waiting to be shot at or got at. I mean, who has ever heard of the great comedians and gifted actors of Leeds, Birmingham or Nottingham, the football fanatics and champions of Southampton, Portsmouth and Oxford, or the top of the chart musicians and pop groups of Carlisle, Norwich and Ipswich?

From Cornwall to Aberdeen nobody has as strong a cultural identity as a Scouser, not even a capital 'cor blimey' Cockney. And there lies the main reason why people from other places delight in taking aim. It's an easy target – something they think they know well. For a lot of Scousers it's something to revel in and laugh about because, after all, it's hardly going to raise an eyelid when you start to take a humorous pot shot at the likes of Stoke or Bristol or Reading. If Liverpool is full of your typical 'bleeding Scousers' then I don't know what the three cities above are full of other than a few Stoke Potters, cider-drinking Bristols, and er, Reading Readers, or is it Reading-ites? Excuse my ignorance, but their cultural identities just don't ring any distinctive ding dong bells. OK, hang on it's Bristolians I think. And did you know that Scouser William Roscoe was once held up as an example to the people of Bristol, who were encouraged to be more like him? But who or what are they famous for? I mean, even with your overly tattooed Geordies up in Newcastle, I can't think of another strikingly familiar trait to take aim at, other than it once took me two hours to read one who was sunbathing in a pair of Speedo ball-stranglers on a Tenerife beach!

From hunger, passion and going without comes the need to feed, want and get. No clearer was this fact shown than during the mid-80s when the need to work, allied to the need to dance, live and love got rationed and starved to the city's population, as they became the target of Tory henchmen wanting to kill off the rebellious spirit of all mass groups of nonconformists, before driving their greed policies and equity stake into the hearts of all the British public. Their 'you too can become a shareholder, house-owner and landowner, or Range Rover-driving stakeholder like us' selling point was sold en masse to a grateful, land-grabbing British public, but meantime 'driven home' to an unaccepting greater Liverpool populace who, I'd like to think, were thinking more along the lines of 'community, not monetary' and 'sod-it, not profit'.

By acting typically un-English, by not going along with the late 70s/ early 80s grand scheme of things, that greed was good and monopoly and privatization are great games to join in with, they quickly became pariahs in capitalist quarters. A legacy and often a burden we still live with today. But the rest of the British people were sold on the idea, and that was that! Anyway, concerning rebellion and saying NO, face it, the majority of the English people were always a bit 'too English' in comparison, and I mean, how do you keep a good greed salesman down? And isn't that what all good Tories basically are?

It's a good feeling for me to think that for a short while Liverpool as a city tried to tell the wolf at the door to stick his stolen pocket watch collection back inside his golf club blazer and 'fuck right off'. But, and it's a big Billy goat of a butt, Liverpool was never going to win against the super-rich Tory party, the Tory media and the Tory population. To all those pockets of people around the country (Greenham Common, large parts of Manchester and other working cities who couldn't be bought, the miners etc.) who stood firm against greed and privatization, Liverpool salutes you. In a world where people will bend more subserviently and more often than Freddie Mercury in a Turkish steam room, and the vast majority want it all and they want it now, they, like Liverpool, never stood a chance. But at least they stood. The salesmen and women played and continue to play on that selfish psyche, till we have ended up with the world their credit card companies and the swipers have created today. Communist and Socialist regimes have bitten the dust and continue to be swiped away as we speak, as the capitalist in all of us screams out for more McDonalds, more Versace and more, more, more.

Where will it end? In a full-circle capitalist oblivion of course, where people think they have everything but deep down feel they have nothing. In the nations of the well-to-do, the North Americas, the Western Europes and the Australias, we're most of the way there already aren't we? But 'Beware' signs are already in order because a billion Russian, Asian, South American and African people are watching TV and internet screens as we read this, all wanting their slice, and troubled times are looming for the capitalist theorists and benefactors, as a world unable to sustain the constant growing demand rears its ugly head over a new designer horizon. It's road-rage spooky. All about getting there fast and me, me, me! But for some mad reason, Liverpool, a place that still houses a lot of nonconformists, makes me feel safe. Mad, I know, but there you go.

Being the European Capital of Culture, Liverpool in boxing terms, on the scale of size and stature, would probably be referred to as a tip-top welterweight compared to the likes of heavyweight London, Paris and Barcelona; but being a city that has always punched above its weight culturally, and in terms of being 'on the map', Liverpool fights like a heavyweight. Not economically but without doubt culturally. This is due in no small part to the restless creativity of its natives. Concerning writers, musicians and artists in general does any other city of its size in Europe have such a concentrated gathering of artists unlimited? I think not.

Throughout the days of Thatcherism (mainly the early 80s) when heavyweight London had most of the North and specifically Liverpool in an economic stranglehold, and flooring blows of company closure after company closure were landed on a weekly basis, the populist majority, almost down and out, soon found a way to talk themselves back up again – back from the brink. Liverpool really does have a remarkable fighting spirit. Witnessed gloriously when their sporting heroes made the most memorable comeback that top-flight football has ever witnessed in Istanbul 2005. The Scouse supporters never-say-die attitude won that one undoubtedly for me, and anyone who knows the difference between Bolton Wanderers' ex-manager, Anne Robinson, and, once again, the Weakest Link's Sammy Lee would surely agree – 'And there's to you Mrs. Robinson…'

Most places need to be economically sound or maybe even boom before artistic venture is celebrated, attempted, or for it to become known or successful. With Liverpool it's as though the opposite effect takes place. As the place was virtually brought to its knees it was as though people became more insular and turned to their own arts and sports scene to help revive flagging spirits. As riots took place and picket lines were drawn and hardship became the norm, musical groups, writers and artists sprang from Hope Eternal Street in numbers not seen since the swinging, booming sixties, while the footballers and their supporters delighted in showing the rest of the country how it was to be played and sung. Financial prospects were not good, but artistically TV companies and theatres spawned dramas and plays by writers who became household names: *Educating Rita*, Willy Russell, *Boys from the Blackstuff*, Alan Bleasdale, while musicians penned songs about riots – 'Piggy in the Middle Eight' by local heroes Cook Da' Books, and political songs like 'Tramp the Dirt Down' by Elvis Costello, about what he'd like to do to Margaret Thatcher's grave once she made her final exit.

I lived through those times. They affected me. Two major redundancies without hope of further employment filled me with a stubborn determination to do something about my plight. Others, not so strong-willed, plugged in hi-fis and got stoned, or guitars and took to heavier drugs and paid the ultimate price. I, like thousands of other local people, lost friends and neighbours through London government economic policy. It's something you don't forget easily – if ever. Looking at things in perspective, I fought back and continue to do so. All Liverpool people need to do is look within themselves for that creative fighting spirit. Look within, and find a way. Whether it is cultural, entrepreneurial or indomitable, I know that they have what it takes. If we do it in number, we need never find ourselves back in the economically deprived mid-80s again.

Those times were the making or breaking of a lot of people. A lot of those forced onto the dole and into the social security system opted to emigrate to Australia, New Zealand, the States or Canada, while thousands took the simpler yet still difficult move of settling somewhere else in and around the UK. Many found work and settled, while thousands lived in digs from Monday to Friday wherever employment was found, before returning home for well-earned weekend breaks. After the Nazi-like Stormin' Norman Tebbit made his famous 'they'll have to get on their bikes' retort to mass unemployment in the area, Scouse enclaves grew quickly in places like snooty Bournemouth, cold London, lovely Jersey and tranquil yet unexciting Torquay, and further afield in fantastic Frankfurt, sunny Santa Monica and the dive that is called Amsterdam. I went to Bournemouth, London and Jersey for building work. I even jumped aboard a plane to South Africa, a place I detested once I got there. Socialist upbringing apart, I was unsure of what awaited me in the gold-mining city of Johannesburg.

If I went with eyes half-open due to being on the bones-of-my-arse and unemployed, I returned a year later with eyes wide-open but still on the bones-of-my-arse. I'd have happily returned home after a month but I had to work to get my air fare and African keep in pocket. I'm glad I stayed, because, factamundo: 'you never know a place till you live there'. A lot of the *Sun* and *News of the World* reading British public could try that old adage concerning my hometown. If I thought Thatcher and her henchmen were 'bang-on' the right wing then the South Africans were so far off to the right side of the waterlogged pitch that they'd sailed right over the edge of the world in a whiter than white Christopher Columbus boat called the good ship SS. If myself and the other Liverpool lads working there had left Speke Airport thinking that, along with the usual Irish, Scousers were the new niggers of Great Britain, and we did, and we were, then we never really knew the true meaning of the word till we lived in white-on South Africa.

With hindsight, and only through lack of funds, I'm glad I stayed put to see the modern-day Nazis in action. Want to educate yourself all about your real enemy? Keep your head down and go and live in his back garden. One thing I couldn't handle, which stays with me to this day, is visiting the chippy for lunch (yeah, the Nazis had chippies) and being told to come to the front of the queue by the white owner; ignoring him to stand in line; then being told by the black people waiting that as a Boss-man I should go directly to the front like the other Boss-man had just told me. Shows what systematic and institutionalized racism can do to poor people. As a humorous footnote: front of the queue in right-on South Africa, back of the queue in snooty Bournemouth. Funny what blonde hair and blue eyes could do for you in a dirty, stinking right-wing country, where accent and look were thought of only as... English?

If I ever had a racist bone in my body it was due to lack of learning and teaching during my time in and under the British education system. I had one big laugh and no hard time in my looney-tunes school, but thing is, they'll teach you all about King Tut and how he chopped off everybody's head because they wouldn't let him start a new religion, and how he kept chop, chop, chopping because certain ladies of the day couldn't or wouldn't have babies to him. Or about the Great British Empire that was rightfully land-grabbed and stolen from unequal heathens by her Majesty's armies in the name of God, Queen and country. Or how you'll have your arse smacked or hands caned and strapped if you don't learn all about Latin, algebra and logarithms, oh yeah. But, and again it's that big Billy goat of a butt, would they shite teach you about equality, different races and religions and the fact that large ethnic minority groups were settled and living just down the road from me and mine in Toxteth, no more than a mile from the Mersey. If I hardly knew the mix-and-match-up of places in my own city, then I was taught zilch about the slave traders who'd come to Liverpool to carpetbag a quick buck before pissing off out as soon as slavery was abolished, and only snippets about British and ex-British colonies like Rhodesia and South Africa.

Though my Dad would walk me through the Pierhead and tell me bits and bobs about boats full of slaves in chains, it was as though I had to go all the way to Johannesburg to learn about the evil machinations of the slave trade. I was given some historical enlightenment by a co-working Christian Sowetan called Samuel who gratefully chanced losing his shitty, menial employment to give me the low-down on 'his' country, my country, and the abomination called slavery. There it is, on my doorstep, and all I'm getting told is Lord and Lady Haw Haw this and British Empire that and how logarithms, algebra and Latin would one day make sense and get me a mortgage and a car – Ha! My ancestors were not even thinking about taking the boat from Ireland and other parts of Europe to Liverpool while slavery was a daily part of Liverpool life. For that reason alone, myself and my own feel no collective guilt about its filthy chained-up history. Saying that, I still would have liked to have been taught all about it in school – fucking algebra! Huh!

Before you know the difference between a white South African and Thatcher, a mathematical fraction and a religious faction, and the British Empire and the Empire theatre, you've left school and are bang in the wheel. You're one of the fresh, new hamsters running around the cage not knowing where the hell you're going, what you're supposed to do to get there, while worrying daily about some new job you're about to start but don't want to do. As I left school and the Tories came to power I thought the best way to get by was to really not give a shit! Yeah, that was my 'early leaving day's' philosophy. Don't think too deeply and it'll all sort itself out.

At sixteen, like most school leavers, I was thinking about football and money, girls and ale and clothes and music, roughly in that order. Within two years I was heavily politicized by everything that was kicking off around me. Less ships in the river, more empty factories, large queues outside the dole and social welfare offices. Next thing, people are emigrating in number, communities disbanding, I'm thinking of 'the off' myself but don't really want to leave (football, family and humour made up my anchor). Then, threatened with redundancy, I really started to take notice of the politics of life all around me. My father was a shop steward at AC Delco and lost his job. My mother was a dinner lady and lost hers. All around people were joining the dole queues and feeling the pinch. Suddenly from being a happy-go-lucky teenager I'm watching the news more often because people in the street are talking about redundancy and being skint. For the first time in my life I listened to people like Thatcher, Tebbit and Lord Whitelaw and they disgusted me with their lecherous faces and insincerity which, at the time, was absolutely obvious to me.

Soon as they started rattling on about greed is good and you need to think about having loadsa-money and getting on the property ladder and becoming a bit of an equity secretary, and that privatization is good and you too can play the shareholder and buy shares and share in the profits from coal, gas, oil, water, fresh air etc, etc, etc, I knew, I mean, I just knew the sons and daughters of Thatcher would one day come home to roost... then multiply and eventually drown us in an ocean of debt, get and a 'whatever you do the mortgage must be met' mentality. Telling us we could all be pop stars, media moguls and top-o-the-ladder entrepreneurs, and that we could all be players and movers and shakers, because, after all, that's what we really, really, deep down in our hearts all wanted. I knew the capitalist doctrine and way of thinking never took into consideration people's true personalities.

The fact that the majority of the population hadn't got a clue about how to become rich, were not really that bothered about changing their lives to be so, or, in most cases, simply didn't have the genetic makeover to be real, real go-getters like the Richard Bransons, Alan Sugars and Rupert Murdochs of this world, seemed in my young estimation to get totally overlooked. Steely-eyed ruthlessness in becoming the Billy-big-bollocks at the top of the corporate ladder is definitely not a trait bestowed on all of us – let alone a tenth of us. And, that my friend, is where right-on capitalism will always fail the human race. That and the fact that the majority of the movers and shakers don't let their wealth trickle down to the masses, no, they keep it locked up all for themselves.

Now let's get it right, this capitalist gravy train is a bit of a hedonistic, moneybags ride while you're on it – part of it – but, fact is, like your best ecstasy-swallowing, cocaine-snorting Ibizan disco-dancer it's always going to get derailed and fall down that steep hill to oblivion... isn't it? It's as inevitable as it is absolutely unsustainable. See, while there are Beverley Hills benefactors walking gold-paved streets carrying Louis Vuitton bags full of dosh, and Surrey stock-brokers driving Rolls Royces with diamond-plated, Prada-logoed steering wheels, and pop stars with homes that require seven walk-in wardrobes to house their 300-strong training shoe collection, then, flipside, there will be thousands of Third World miners, mechanics and sweatshop workers all struggling to get by in their daily lifestyle routines. There will be victims. I was taught these things from an early age, and though most kids had next to nothing where I lived, most of them had morals and bags of respect for other human beings. Well let me state the obvious: Not any more Pedro!

Therein lies the reason why I'm telling you all this, and what made me proud of my city, Liverpool. The actual fact that here, for a short space in time, was a place that turned its back on the Conservative theory of greed is healthy and greed is good, and took the humane stance of 'fuck you and your walking all over the weak and ordinary people of this world, because one day your vacuous, materialistic viewpoint will jump track and crash and burn and take millions overboard with it'. And don't let me romanticize too much here because, yes, Liverpool in all its pomp and glory had always been a Tory stronghold. But that was where the education from elders about history and past came in. Throughout the pomp and glory days of being the Empire's second city Liverpool's general populace had always been kept on starvation rations and in the background when the gold coins and fat turkeys were getting handed out.

You need to know your history to not let 'cap-in-hand' times be forced upon you all over again. I truly believe your average Scouser knows his city history a lot more than the average UK citizen. And in our city the whole story of the rise and fall of capitalism is right there in front of your face, crack-bang in your everyday life. Put simply: to read the story of the rise and fall of capitalism, read the history of Liverpool. Due to ill treatment in the past, whether it was back in famine-ridden Ireland, Wales, Scotland or Africa, or the forcing of casual labour on a dock workforce, or no improvement in the quality of life during the days of pomp, Liverpool people didn't forget. Not mine anyway. The mistreatment and consistent abuse of the general populace here and around the rest of the world by a thoroughly ruthless British aristocracy, especially throughout the days of building of Empire, is a well-documented historical fact. And like the Celtic football song, 'If y'know y'history, it's enough to make y'heart go wo-oh-oh-oh!'

Liverpool didn't ignore the humane part of our nature, the suicidal mothers and wives of striking miners and dockers, the communities that were torn apart and blitzed worse than Hitler's boys had ever managed, and the poisoning of our environment with factory chemicals that were the slimy end of all that 'greed is good' theory. The legacy of which is here as we speak: the Sonnae factory in Kirkby for instance, which spews out sawdust and woodchips into the chests and lungs of the local residents daily. No, Liverpool for a short time in British political history stuck two fingers up and said 'fuck you and trying to grab at your runaway bullion rattler'.

But, suppose like any runaway train that will flatten all in its path, till one day it meets an immovable force – a body of people or matter that is so strong that it forces the train to crash and disintegrate into the dust – that runaway rattler will hurtle on into the distance, destroying all in its way and wake, leaving casualties untold. And face it, a lot of the youth of today's Liverpool have pulled up their hoods and the powers that be have ironed their suits and honed their acts, and both scurried aboard. It's turned within the space of twenty years from the humane, 'Are you alright Jimmy?', to the more self-righteous 'I'm alright Jack'. So welcome my friend, welcome to Liverpool 2008, the new millennium, where the Labour government has said if you can't stop the greed-is-good rattler, then you'd better jump aboard sharpish, and most of today's youth, terrified of missing out, have bought a ticket and are praying that they're allowed on. Because I mean, life's not really worth living without owning your own flat and an American Express card, is it? Well, throw in this year's new digital 'Got to Have' and a 4x4, and I'll ask again: is it? And listen, I know this is supposed to be about the culture thing and 2008 but you have to know where today's culture has recently arrived from and how it was shaped.

Thatcher's legacy has been to see this country descend into the selfish society we see around us today, where whole groups of young people feel alienated and disenfranchised, while others, less numbered, have wealth and prospects and, therefore, do not. I mention her and her government frequently because today we see the results of all that she and her creed selfishly taught and created. Again, put simply: Selfishness! People are yet again ignoring history in the sprint for material wealth. It's the haves and have-nots all over again, and vast gangs of youths are roaming council estates with no understanding or respect for the lives and property of others. Some will say that is the nature of the beast, but it's as though the 'greed is good' motto and selfishness have been daubed upon their souls and they want a piece of the action and cake and they want it like Robbie Williams and Paris Hilton and the Spice Girls all rolled into one, and they want it instantly! No busking the streets for years, no learning the chords, no dying on stage in the clubs where stardom apprenticeships were plied. Concerning apprenticeships of any sort – who's got the time or patience? Concerning listening to people who live in areas about to be regenerated, who has got the time to truly listen? Nah, it's all X-factor instant glory without the back-up story.

With the emphasis on possessions and academic achievement,

where successive governments have encouraged people to fight only for self, while family values become secondary, it is no wonder ordinary folk feel intimidated by roaming gangs of hoodies on the make or on the take. But as I was saying, for one small moment in time people with Liverpool DNA, who knew a little about their history, took a Custer's last stand, only to be shot down and ridiculed by a nation paying lip service to a Tory media, a capitalist theory and the thought that one day they too could be millionaires.

By now you'll have realized that I'm very proud to come from Liverpool: the mongrel city where blood from all corners of the world has been mixed and spilled and glory-be to that, because if inter-bred means you end up looking like Prince Charles or Camilla (is Paul Daniels the royal magician?) then I'm off to Cream in Alaska to get me an Eskimo girlfriend right away. As a service to the rest of the tea and scones brigade and any of the visiting Great British public, the main reason I'm telling you all this is to reach the point where I'll try to compile what the DNA make-up of a typical Liverpool person really is... Well, I am at that point, so without further...

Liverpool DNA

Nicky Allt

OK – Starting off in mongrel-tough Mother Mary Ellen's loins – Scouse DNA includes all of the following:

1: The Mersey – it has played such a significant part in the branching of our family trees and in the city's history that it runs through our bodies alongside blood and bone. It's the salt in our Scouse and the salt on our chips.

2: Immigration. We are an immigrant city with mainly Irish, a lot of Welsh, Scots, some English, then Italian, Norwegian, Chinese, German, Russian and a host of African nations' blood running through our veins. If you are Liverpudlian by birth and not all of the above run through you, then at least you'll be definitely made up of part of. With certain districts the blood count of one or two nations can go higher. But, couple of districts apart, like it or not, this is genetic Liverpool life.

3: We are aware of the fact that we are all part of a great musical heritage that began in other countries but got finely honed on the banks of our own River Mersey. Recently named as the 'World Capital of Pop' by the *Guinness Book of Hit Singles*, Liverpool has produced more Number 1 hits per capita than any other city on the planet. Fifty-four Number 1's apparently. If we were the 51st state of America we'd probably be called 'Nashville by the sea', with glorified guitar-themed Disneylands abounding. We have musical melody and entertainment in our make-up. It's in our bones to want to sing and dance and tell stories. An endless list of bands, comedians, actors and artists in general who have graced screen and stage are testimony to that. For as near a take on defining that pure, pure 'Liverpool Sound' check out the Beatles 'I Feel Fine' or the La's 'Feeling'.

4: We have a history of political unrest and social upheaval second to none, due to our being a dockside port looking out to sea for trade and inspiration, and due to our immigrant nature being in turmoil or disagreement with the ruling London classes. From dock strikes and Churchill wanting to put his navy warships in the Mersey with guns trained on Liverpool, and Militant Labour taking on the Thatcherites in the eighties, and Maggie and her economic henchmen targeting the city as Public Enemy No.1, we are a rebellious Celtic enclave on the north-west tip of an Anglo-Saxon kingdom.

5: We are usually generous and giving of spirit, as seen in the pulling together of our communities during times of tragedy on numerous occasions (Hillsborough, little Rhys Jones and James Bulger). This gets misunderstood as being over-sentimental or mawkish by the rest of uninterested, stiff-upper-lip Britain – till Lady Dianna dies and we see a public outpouring of mass grieving never witnessed on these shores before, except… maybe by Liverpool.

6: We are too in-your-face. We are not conformist or subservient when it comes to doffing the cap when the jobs are getting handed out by y'Lords and y'Ladies of industry, resulting in Liverpool often being bottom of the list when a multinational corporate company needs to open a new branch in the UK. This can be traced back to casual labour on the docks when men had to go cap-in-hand for work, otherwise their families often went without. From the near-revolutionary Dock and General Transport strike of 1911 and those days forward, when people like my grandparents fought for an end to that system, the man on the street has a built-in non-submissive nature concerning bosses and employers.

7: We are often cynical due to what has gone on in the past. The summing up of Liverpool people's flippantly cynical nature could be put this way. You tell a group of Liverpool residents that great times and prosperity are on their way to the city, they'll say, 'Don't think so mate, it'll never happen around here.' You tell the same set of people that the worst times ever are just around the corner and they'll offer, 'Ah, don't worry mate, it'll all work out just fine, you'll see.' This stubborn cynicism, out of line with Southern ruling-class trends, comes from knowing your history, ignoring countrywide vogues and inclinations and not giving a hoot about what the rest of the nation says.

8: We can be seriously insular and mistrustful of outsiders who promise good tidings, and sceptical or even downright jealous of our own number who try to be different or do things in their own way – sometimes Liverpudlians have to leave Liverpool to be successful, before eventually being accepted back as a victorious son of the city. 'You put your head above the parapet in this town and there's a thousand opinionated critics all waiting to have a pop.' Shame, but there you go!

9: We love sport. It starts in the playground: Catlick vs. Proddy-dog, North end vs. South end (not important nowadays and rightly so); red or blue; British Bulldog or Allaleeyo; toy fights or shoulders; pair knockout or three-and-in; 60 seconds or spot; football; boxing; athletics; you name it, we're competitive and up for a gamble, and a game!

10: It is a hard, edgy city. It's dock-located shipping history, people of un-English origin and rabble-rousing politics make up a heady mix, and people have never been afraid to air their grievances out on the street. At the weekend it sometimes feels like a frontier town – a cowboy town. If you go around thinking you are the big-square-cheese then soon enough somebody is going to treat you to the old Cheddar gorge by taking a bite out of you till you become a little ol' triangular Dairylea once again. Big square means: big head, shoulder pads and a ten-gallon hat. Little triangle means: normal head and sloping shoulders with a 'told-off' demeanour, bit like the average naked man after a cold shower. Remember: show us your heart and don't act the Billy Big Bollocks!

11: Excuse me if number eleven is long but we love to have a laugh more than any other city or its people I've ever visited or met; and sometimes at the expense of anyone or anything, including ourselves. It's like a form of cutting black humour at times and often surreal to the max. For me, it's like a little tap you turn on at will whenever you need to let off steam, or simply laugh at the absurdity of everyday life. Often Liverpool people will laugh at serious misfortune, even at the expense of others as though it's no big deal, or at things others don't find amusing at all.

Sometimes, I'm sorry, but you just can't help yourself. Like the time I was stood in the queue for a water-ski ride at the Wet and Wild theme park on International Drive in Orlando, Florida. Being the middle of summer I stood waiting in line for a set of skis and handlebars that pulled you around a lake at speed, as long as you had balance and could hold on for dear life. The idea was to stay on for as long as possible, especially after waiting such a long time to ride. The handlebars were attached to a huge overhead pulley that wired itself around the lake, being held up by telegraph poles set evenly at intervals outside the lake circumference.

You had to be up and on your marks when your turn came, as a lifeguard held you vertically, moments before this thing flew from the safety trap. Determined not to make a mess at take-off (back of the 20-minute queue if you did) I studied the riders, trying to pick up any skiing tips. Stood in front of me was a huge 25-stone American woman, who after several tries informed me she now had the technique off to a fine art, adding that her size and weight were a great anchor in giving her a balanced ride around most of the lake. In other words: no puny water-park ride could give her trouble any more. She was an American; she had to show everyone she was the biggest and best at keeping afloat.

The ride looked quite dangerous and I was surprised there was no insurance waiver to sign seeing as the Yanks are all sue-crazy. Noticing my concern she offered insight into how it was done and a number of tips for a good take-off – the make or break part of the ride. Watching intently as the guard struggled to hold her huge frame upright, she gave me a thumbs-up and a 'know-all, watch-me-go' wink seconds prior to launch. As a set of handlebars came around and she gripped on tightly, her Velcro safety gloves and XXL lifejacket in place, the lifeguard let go and the key word here is launch. As he did so, the lady flew out of the skis, out of her lifejacket, and after travelling horizontally through the air for ten metres, smacked the water like a speedboat that just flew off the top of a tsunami wave. The smack as she hit the water must've been heard in Bootle library as she smashed into the lake surface three or four times, completing at least a quarter of the lake in bounce-mode. The lifeguard set an alarm off and the ride came to a juddering stop.

People queuing looked shell-shocked and voices muttered 'no-way Jose', as they drifted out of line. Meanwhile, cruel I know, but chuckling away, I couldn't help myself. At first I tried holding it in, but looking at my mate stood ten places back, we burst out laughing. That was it, we were off. By now the lifeguard had swum around and dragged the blubbering American lady out of the lake. As he threw a lifebelt over her, my mate called out 'He's just thrown a doughnut over a doughnut', and we were off again. Though undoubtedly shaken and shocked, her arms and legs were all in place. As he helped her onto dry land, I thought of the wink, then the smack, and a glove and a lifejacket flying into the air and couldn't stop myself again and again. My mate in line was laughing more than me, as he pointed at the people staring at us, and then the unfortunate disbelieving lady. One or two couldn't resist a wry smile, but we were laughing out loud in fits and starts. Once we were back with the rest of our gathering we had to lie down on sunbeds as they tried to find out what was so funny. We were in absolute bulk.

There's definitely not much sympathy knocking about in Liverpool humour I can tell you. If you're ugly you'll get told: 'Eh mate, why don't yer rob a bank a day, cos wearing a stocking over yer head each morning is a definite improvement on that'; 'Ah ay lad, you must be two-faced, cos I tell yer, you've gorra cheek walking the streets with that one'; 'Tell yer what mate, you've got a face that only a boxer's glove could love'. In short, you have a face like a well-used tea bag, a window cleaner's sponge or a baboon's arse. If you're a big woman, you'll get asked: 'You gorra big, fat set of flabby thighs down there girl, cos I can't tell with yer belly already covering them?' 'How's it feel getting upholstered every morning sweetheart?' And, 'Scuse me girl, is your name the Isle of Man?' Or you'll get told: 'Bet that car of yours has got stretch marks. Eh love, what are yer doing with a packet of hot dogs on yer neck?'

If you're scruffy you might get asked: 'I bet your undies are older than Jennifer Ellison'. 'They don't half look comfy those car seat covers!' And, 'How come you've wrinkled yer clothes and ironed yer face?' For the following afflictions you may hear any of these. Hairy: 'Are you the bastard lovechild of John Travolta and a Dennis Healey eyebrow!' Big nose: 'Has that got its own spine?' Bad teeth: 'You a Sugar Puff advert?' Promiscuous: 'Ah eh love, introduce yer right leg to yer left leg will yer, it's not fair that they've never met!' Ugly and promiscuous: 'Bet it paid a few quid being on the cover of that Smackhead boot weekly!' Lazy: 'Do you hitch hike when yer sleepwalk?' Big glasses: 'Can you see into the future with those gigs?' Skinny: 'Our dog would love to bury you in the garden!'

While an endless stream of insults can be a way of keeping your feet on the ground – ask any local celebrities – this form of sardonic humour can bury your tootsies in sandstone if you're on the receiving end of too many blows for comfort, or for too long. Meaning: time to escape! A lot of Liverpool stars piss off first million, usually to London or abroad. Nine-to-five executive types, of a more sensitive nature, not on board with giving and taking 'a dig', can often be seen fleeing to the distant hills of woollybackland; places like Chorley, Widnes and Wigan, or even as far as Manchester and Yorkshire. On a positive: they leave behind the dreaded whip of the nasty Scouse tongue. On a negative: in so doing their children often inherit the even worse woollyback disease of not getting the ale in!

Key Words

1: Mersey

2: Immigrants

3: Artistic

4: Political

5: Generous

6: Nonconformist

7: Cynical

8: Insular

9: Sporting

10: Edgy

11: Sarky Humour

CATCH YER LATER!

Artist's view ...

Art in a City

Anthony Brown

✥

Tony Brown is an artist, graphic designer and musician who I have the utmost respect for. Not only for the brilliance of his talent, but for his 'discipline in perseverance' in seeing through to the finish the glorious '100 Heads Thinking As One' project. Including all the plays, shows and presentations that 2008 will bring, this is the finest exhibition you could go to see. Not seen it yet? Get yer flabby arse in gear and go see something just a little bit special. When I first viewed the ocean of life that Tony had created, stood high atop the steps of St George's Hall, well... what words can I say, you know, that will do one man's creativity justice... I'm getting the goose-bumps now, so without rattling any further I'll have a bash at one. It's the only one that travels quickly down the tubes... Gobsmacked! Yeah, that's the one.

Liverpool is a city built on the foundations of culture and unique-ness, a fact that we all take for granted as we grow, walk and talk through a life here. My problem with that? We have never needed a middle man to tell us the greatness of our art, our stories, our act, our sport and our wit, but the grave mistake all those years ago was to entrust our gift to people of far lesser talents and ambition well above their capabilities. This is not a present-day argument against a Culture Committee, no, for me the damage was created long before the millen-nium hit town. Our mistake was allowing mediocre people a position of authority. Arts and cultural spokespeople who would not know a pencil from a spade and whose barking criticism, self-righteous babble and patronizing, moronic ideal of 'High Art' has relentlessly kicked the support from underneath those who have needed it most. Yes, many have risen above these obstacles but most of them have had to hone their craft away from Liverpool's boundaries and return bringing with them the applause and respect of those who have appreciated their gift.

I'm proud to be a son of generations of Liverpudlians and as the world's spotlight shines on us I unfold my wish for 2008. My hope is that the charlatans and professional chancers who have connived and bullshitted a position, purporting to be a voice on our behalf, will stand and be discounted, admit their lack of vision due to the stars in their eyes, round up the one-trick ponies and all whose heads and hearts lack a single original thought, and fuck right off – leaving the stage clear for the mass of creative and positive thought from all those who will illuminate not only our 'Culture Year' but our many ground-breaking, city-shaking, global vibrating years to come.

Liverpool = food for life.

Liverpool life ...
Outsourced Liverpool

Steve Higginson

❧❧

Steve Higginson is a writer, film maker and ex-postal union official who is co-author with Tony Wailey of the Edgy Cities – Take a Walk on the West Side *photo exhibition. Like a lot of us, Steve has been heavily politicized by his Liverpool life. I met Steve at* Brick up the Mersey Tunnels *one night, and understood his own form of Liverpool lingo instantly. Telling me of his love of DJ Sneak, Aretha Franklin and Boca Juniors, Steve talks edgy and writes edgy, and that I found likeable from the off. I asked him to write a piece for this book and he dropped me this superb little account of how he views the point where politics and culture collide in this, his city...*

I have been trying to think when I first realized that politics and culture do not mix. I'm sitting in our house and there is an 18-page newspaper pull-out about French cultural life. Page after page of art, books, film etc. and there is not a single mention or comment from any politician. The French tradition of *liberté* in all aspects of life was aimed at keeping out all state interference at local and national levels. Then it dawned on me. Back in the seventies a feller was trying to persuade me about the glories of the Russian Revolution. I was never enamoured. My inherent anarchistic impulse has never sat well with being told what to do and/or being ordered around. My doubts and fears were finally confirmed when I was researching about Marlon Brando and the film *On the Waterfront*. In one of the books there was a description of 1930s New York. The city had become the epicentre of a multi-layered cultural revolution. Popular culture was being made and accessed for and by New York's working class. No longer would they have to rely on a high form of culture being passed down from an elitist cabal.

Into this teeming cauldron of working-class expression and culture, and dressed like a bag of rags, enters one of the leaders of the

Russian Revolution. He is visiting New York for the first time. His only previous life experience was studying the minutiae of a Petrograd pin factory. And how does he address the assembled throng, all awaiting his pearls of wisdom? He begins with 'Workers and peasants of Harlem and the Bronx...' (Is there anyone left on the planet who still wonders why working-class people have never bothered with revolutionary politics?)

So politics and culture always need to be kept separate. We should always be aware about their different effects. Politicians deal in economic and financial relationships. Economic development does not welcome autonomous cultural development. Only cultural creativity that subsumes itself to a rigid economic and financial discipline is ever acceptable. In Liverpool today we are witnessing the birth of a favoured and elitist creative class. It is armed with the new credo of economic growth through 'cultural creativity'. But its creativity is focused solely upon non-inclusive economic initiatives.

For the credo to work there has to be a climate created for outside investment, accompanied by outside creative talent. The consequences, intended or not, are that external creative talent replaces local innovation/talent. Otherwise the inward capital flow is irrelevant. Cultural capital is mobile (here today and gone tomorrow). Because of the mobility of investment, the control of public space becomes crucial.

We have been working on *Edgy Cities: Take a Walk on the Westside*, filming Liverpool as a city of the imagination, as a 'place of space'. But try and find Liverpool as a space. Walking the city, what unfolds before your eyes is the privatization of public space. No longer can we access those long Liverpool streets, north and south, that sloped down to the river where land and sea melted into one, where you could see those huge Liverpool/Atlantic skies. Having removed people from the river's edge and moved them inland, the final phase is enacted through the elimination of the river from any public view, similar to when you used to go the match or to a concert – tickets for restricted views. Our seaburbia spectacle is now limited as a full river view is only for the wealthy few.

The discipline of waterfront planning is removing the waterfront's soul. Waterfront planning is programmed to pin down space into a single and static entity (no entry and no exit). The spontaneous and casual uses people make in their daily routines around the riverfront are being severely limited with new boundaries appearing each week. I never knew a riverbank area could be outsourced. Very soon the words

'I need my own space' will be defunct coz where can you go if the city is full of No Entry/Exit signs? The waterfront is becoming an (elite) *Quarterfront*, with *quarter* being the operative word as it represents what will be left of the city for the rest of us to inhabit.

Questions about the urban strategies whereby Liverpool is being re-defined are becoming increasingly pointless. Who do you address the questions to? The lines between municipal agencies, national architects and translational organizations have become increasingly blurred so there is no public accountability. Liverpool is controlled by a number of inter-related quangos. We are living under a quangocracy – with quangocrats wielding huge amounts of power in determining Liverpool as a place of space

Like anyone, I can be 'haunted by the past'. It is a common-place phrase because it's a commonplace experience. Even if we are not strictly 'haunted', the past is always with us because it shapes our present, and the older you get the longer your past grows... but looking around Liverpool today the presence of my past is becoming longer and stronger. Liverpool postal workers have walked out on unofficial action at the same time as we are trying to get images of the Merseyside Trade Union and Unemployed Community Centre on Hardman Street. Some students from LIPA have organized a protest inside and outside the building. We are filming it as our reminder and a trace of Liverpool history. It was a place where I worked when I was an anarchic postal union official. Of a night, Upstairs at the Picket was my cultural edge. The building shaped every aspect of my life. Why is it not a listed building? It has now been sold off for luxury flats. As if Liverpool needed any more. The New Picket has been re-located to a city periphery and God knows how many stairs it takes to get there now.

History is not just about remembering but is also about forgetting. So filming outside the now derelict building, the day the Liverpool postal workers were on strike, meant our photography became a series of time loops and time warps where our past, present and future rolls into one.

In the late 1980s I went with a charity brigade to Nicaragua to help save them from the American Imperialists. My local union had a benefit night at the Picket. All the bands were postal workers; the High Five, the Lettermen, other lads who were later the Tambourines. (A prime example of the working class being more than mere production statistics.) Nicaragua was a life-changing experience for me. So much so that the 28 people who went there have barely spoken to each other since we touched down again at Heathrow in 1991. It all started the first week we got there. I was in charge of the musical entertainment. The locals were taken by Steve 'Silk' Hurley and 'Jack Your Body', but we were over-ruled and instead we had folk music by oppressed Norfolk agricultural workers... You can see how it all started to go dreadfully wrong... 28 of us living in an old barn up in the hills of Nicaragua. It did teach me one thing. People of Latin America refer to Americans by their geographical location, North Americans. In Spanish 'north' is 'norte'... So for weeks I listened to tales of woe about 'naughty Americans'... Served me right. I should have learnt Spanish.

Back to my original point. The quangocracy is at its most cretinous when announcing the blueprint for Liverpool waterfront development in order for it to resemble New York. If any of them had the slightest sense of Liverpool history, they would know that back in 1886, Liverpool was described as 'The New York of Europe... A World city rather than a British provincial.' Well over a century ago a London magazine was confirming Liverpool as a different place; a Liverpool which is anywhere and everywhere. It is the reason why Liverpool has always known more about Buenos Aires and New York than about Barnsley and Norwich. It is also why the favourite watering hole of Diego Maradona in the Boca dockside area of Buenos Aires is called the Liverpool Light. You will never find a 'Barnsley Bistro' in Havana will you?

A distinctive feature of Liverpool has been its history of fusing local uniqueness with a global view. Liverpool is *in* the UK but has never been *of* it. It has always belonged to a wider expansive world. Yet it is obvious that there is a subtle shift taking place. The quangocracy might talk the language of inclusion; but in practice they exclude. In a desire to attract cultural capital from outside the city by becoming creatively diverse, local creativity is diverted onto a road to nowhere.

The name of the game is to attract and then retain new talent from outside by ignoring local talent on the inside. So we reach the farcical stage whereby an initiative put together from some local kids gets rejected. Instead preference is given to some Miming Puppet Troupe from Horsham. If the same criteria operated in the 1960s, the Beatles would have been knocked back in favour of Freddie and the Dreamers and Dave Dee, Dozy, Beaky, Mick and Titch.

Remember Liverpool gained the Capital of Culture status because the bid reflected and represented the nature of the city. It gave

Liverpool an 'edge' over British provincial cities. The 'edge' has been blunted. The levels of local exclusion have an air of condescension and contempt linked to 'class'. We are not supposed to make our own culture. Instead we have to sit still until a cultural clique reveals what is to be enjoyed.

What has been unleashed in Liverpool is not new. The idea for the creative-city strategy was devised in America a few years ago. The 'Cool City' programme is where apparent cultural radicalism hides a deeper monetary conservatism. The intention was to provide an engine for economic and social regeneration. On the surface it looks very seductive, until you study the consequences occurring in some of the American cities. Economic and cultural development created its own dynamic, the end state being highly skewed in favour of attracting and retaining a favoured class of 'right on and creative cool people'.

New buzz words were created like 'hipsterization'. City mayors thought it trendy. It was basically selling cities to the highest bidder. New creative elites with their mobile money would then define all aspects of cultural production. Therefore the script for urban cultural regeneration is re-working the methods of a bygone age of industrial society where the means of cultural production/reproduction will be in the hands of a select few.

It seems that our politicians and civic leaders have completely absorbed the concept. This new form of economic regeneration is like a runaway train. The new cultural over-class will create huge costs for the social fabric of the city. Cultural capital and economic inequality are mutually dependent. In American cities there is no longer any obligation to target public resources to socio-economic need. Cities refusing to accept the gentrification of whole areas of public space in order to attract a trendy 'creative' class are simply de-funded – No Go = No Dough!

So a quangocracy drawn from outside the city will be the drivers of our economic and social regeneration. The rest of us will be merely passengers. Our local-global identity is going into reverse to a global-national-local. We are on the bottom rung awaiting with parched lips the trickle down. Welcome to creative-cultural-capital-ism. But don't worry, the circus/McCartney tickets are in the post.

Liverpool was, is, and will always be a city of 'outsiders' who then morph into 'insiders'. It is the reason why the identity of the city is always in flux. Liverpool is an ever-changing same. But we seem to be witnessing a scandal in the making. As a kid I was always told to look for the money trail of the money men. Today as a society, we are geared more and more to watching moving-image forms on mobile phone downloads, on the web and on handheld devices etc.

So let us make sure we do not forget the down-loads, off-loads and mobile money which will very shortly be over and out and leaving behind a legacy of......... unsold cases of 08 mugs. Remember the tag-line from the film, *The Usual Suspects*: 'One Line-Up. No Coincidence'.

2007

Liverpool life ...
Liverpool Lou

Suzanne Collins

-🙐🙒-

Suzanne Collins is a talented person and actress who starred for six years as Nikki Shadwick in Brookside *and is about to perform her third season running as Maggie in* Brick up the Mersey Tunnels. *Her bubbly, infectious nature means she's a joy to work with, and if spirits need lifting among a working group of actors, then Suzanne's the energy and light that gets them working through to the end of the filming day, or to the final lines of a brand new script.*

Being born in Liverpool and brought up in Birkenhead (Mum's family from Birkenhead, Dad's from Liverpool), I feel I belong to both sides of the River. Though I get lots of offers of work away from home, it's home I prefer, as I'm proud to come from this wonderfully creative city of ours. I undoubtedly wouldn't want to live anywhere else, although a bit more sun now and again would be nice (smiles). Sometimes the both sides thing can get in the way though, like with the football, where my Dad supports Liverpool and my brother, Everton. Believe me... I stay well out of that one!

The sense of humour we possess, the accent we speak with and the friendly nature of our people mean Liverpool leaves its mark on you for life. Its not just 'some other place' like a host of capital cities you visit on your travels. Liverpool really is a Cultural Capital with a big double C. With a bouncing nightlife second to none, cathedrals and beautiful buildings abounding, the city not only has its own culture of speech, but moving about the city streets and engaging with its people and places, you'll be on much more than a boring culture walk when you stride through Liverpool. Along with being a hive of activity where artists, writers and musicians can find endless pictures, stories and songs to create, whenever the inspiration arises, the city has an individual feel all of its own. Put it this way: It's different. We're different!

People joining together for a common cause, while still looking out for each other, is a thing we come to expect in this city. This becomes highlighted and more relevant when tragedies like Hillsborough occur, and the same with what happened to beautiful little Rhys Jones. Once tragedies like these happen and the media project them directly into the mind's eye, Liverpool pulls and grieves together. Of course nobody feels it like the families involved, but still we, the city people, feel pain and suffering as one.

Liverpool more than deserves its Capital of Culture status. Whether any good will come of it for the ordinary man in the street is anybody's guess. Only time will tell. But the one thing I know is, given the chance to party nobody can party like us. Let the celebration of our cultural status begin...

2008

Bluecoat view ...
Cultural Cakes and Crevices

Rachael Eades

⋈

Rachael Eades is a marketing officer at the Bluecoat. I first met Rachael when the Bluecoat invited me to a cultural discussion at St George's Hall about whether or not Liverpool thrives due to outsider influence or due to the local Scouse population. Bright and optimistic in her viewpoint, and so she should be for someone 25-ish – ha ha, I like that – she told me she would like to write more often. Her point about her own generation leaving 'their own' legacy is something I fully endorse, in fact, if there were more like her I would get right out of the soddin' way!

A t 25-ish, the mass marketers say that my peers and I straddle generations x and y and just sneak into the latter, making it into the 'young and relevant' box by the skin of our teeth. On hearing this nugget of information I wasn't surprised. The fact that my age group sits in a bit of an uncomfortable cultural crevice is something I've known for a while. You see, I've been feeling a strange ambivalence about my own 'culture' for some time, intensified or maybe even catalysed by the fact that I'm from, live and work in the city set to be European capital of it next year.

I know how lucky we are. How we have never had it so good. Arts organizations in this city like the Bluecoat, FACT, the Everyman and Playhouse, A Foundation, Tate Liverpool, the Royal Liverpool Philharmonic Orchestra, Liverpool Biennial are commissioning and showing an incredibly high standard of international works and are working hard to nurture local artists and audiences through their participation and education programmes. Never before have we been able to enjoy, learn from and be inspired by such a range of artistic output. These organizations are taking an international approach to programming and framing it in a Liverpool setting. It's not here that I feel muddled.

But I do have conflicting feelings about the current climate, the scene from which my generation, us little y-ers, will emerge as the cultural shapers of the forthcoming decades. And do you know what? I think it's because sometimes I (and I'll bet many others of my age and experience) am not actually sure what I want or expect from 'culture' and all that sits under its umbrella. I have a bit of a schizophrenic relationship with it and this city.

Obviously, my wish is to live in an economically prosperous boomtown, full of opportunities, with high levels of employment, standards of education and standards of living. I'm glad that it looks like Liverpool won't become the place I had to leave to make a good living or to find success in my career. (For superstitious people I will endeavour to touch wood as soon as possible.) Same for my children… it would be nice to know that they would quite like it here if I actually had some.

So, as far as I'm aware, to maintain this position and to grow we need businesses to invest in the city and visitors to come and spend their time and money here – yes, mainly their money. And these are the chief civic aims of Liverpool's execution of its year as Capital of Culture. Using art and culture as a driver, Liverpool City Council and Liverpool Culture Company are positioning the city as an international tourism and business destination. Apparently this will make the legacy of 2008 culture-led regeneration, regeneration of our health, education, housing, employment and transport systems through inward spending encouraged by the promotion of the global brand that is Liverpool.

Sounds like a plan.

Indeed, Liverpool does seem to be going through a renaissance of sorts. You know, we are getting a big fat arena and conference centre and Grosvenor have invested millions in developing what seems to me to be a whole new town within town. As I walk around our city centre, this plan to attract inward investment is manifesting itself in glossy retail outlets and chain coffee shops and trendy apartments and bars… lots and lots of bars.

And that's all good right? Because, well, we'll be more like Manchester and Birmingham in a bit won't we? And, you know, people do say that Liverpool is 'ten years behind Manchester' and all that. So, why do I want to say 'Erm hold on a sec, can we just have a little think about this?'

Is it that I just don't like change? Am I in fact being closed minded or sentimental when I start clucking about homogenization and identikit cities? Maybe I am. I could just be being a bit of a Cautious Kate.

In his introduction to the reprint of *Art in a City* by John Willett, Bryan Biggs, Artistic Director at the Bluecoat, makes the point that Liverpool is 'a city that finds itself at the start of the twenty-first century – as it did in the 1960s when the spotlight fell on it in the wake of the Beatles phenomenal global success – with its cultural offer again being scrutinized.' This time, the spotlight isn't on us by some incredible serendipitous sequence of events that meant four lads from Liverpool became the most influential creative force in the world. It has come because we desperately needed to be repackaged and rebranded and that is what our city leaders have set about doing.

So, I'll be honest, I do know that an inherent parochialism is not the reason for my lukewarm response to what I see. I'll reveal my own naive imaginings here (so be gentle with me).

I'm disappointed that 'me and my mates' – my generation of Liverpool dwellers – are not the ones driving this change or the latest reincarnation of Liverpool as the 'centre of the creative universe'. There, I said it. And when it's written down in black and white it does seem a bit petulant – but that's just the way I feel. And I feel justified in mentioning it because I hear it when friends, acquaintances, musicians, artists, taxi drivers and hairdressers of my generation speak.

This disappointment is perverse because I want Liverpool to have its day, but I'm still being a bit of a dissatisfied arse because I want it to happen my way. I remember reading a piece Grayson Perry wrote in *The Times* earlier this year in which he spoke about the 'natural flowering of the Sixties, when artists grew like weeds out of bomb sites and abandoned dockyards'. In the 60s, Liverpool's incredible creative output seemed driven by urban deprivation. Same for the 70s and 80s.

Would I actually want to live in a place like Liverpool in the 70s and 80s with the whole crippling recession, record unemployment thing going on? Definitely not, but (and sorry to be flippant about this) Liverpool in the 70s and 80s, in many ways, sounds pretty cool. I think I'm suffering from rose-tinted glasses syndrome.

Don't get me wrong, dancing around in Heebie Jeebies or La'go in vintage clothes to Dusty or the Buzzcocks is fun, but I doubt anyone there feels like they are part of a cultural revolution. I certainly don't. I instead feel like I'm living in one big pastiche – a big fun pastiche.

I want our own Eric's, a place where musicians, artists, poets and the like get to generate their own subculture, where this subculture can grow organically and us lesser-talented souls can be there, see it happen and in twenty years' time regale some wide-eyed 25-year-old with the stories. But I don't want to just copy all this stuff in the hope that we can create something new and ours by taking, as my new acquaintance Fabian Rothschild puts it, 'stylistic collage approaches, which in reality is tantamount to eclectic plagiarism'.

I don't even know if that's possible. In today's society subculture is gobbled up by mass communication as it emerges, before anyone has time to feel loyalty to it or ownership of it (and herein lies a reason for that uncomfortable cultural crevice-y feeling). This isn't a manifesto. I'm just voicing a confusion and I'm not sure who I'm trying to voice it to. I may in fact just be telling myself off.

I think what I'm really saying is – I want to have my culture cake and eat it. And I make it into the y generation, so I have an excuse.

December 2007

London view ...
Drinking it in

Tony Teasdale

⚑

Tony Teasdale is a magazine editor who now resides in London. I wrote a couple of pieces for him when he was editor at Ice, *a lads' magazine full of topical issues, clobber and footy stories, oh yeah, and loads of naked women – most young lads' ideal reading matter, in truth. He sent me this brief biog...* Anthony Teasdale grew up in suburban Aughton, just north of Liverpool. Useless at anything remotely resembling 'real' work, he has spent the last fifteen years DJ'ing, making music and writing. He currently edits the front section of Arena *magazine which doesn't tax him too much. What a cad!*

Liverpool's at its best when it's not performing for other people's benefit. It works well in the daily interaction between normal people. Not when there's out-of-towners within earshot and the accent is turned to 11, but when it's natural, everyday-like. It's about having a flirt with the woman who sells ciggies and papers or having a moan about the council with the street sweeper who's taken ten minutes to have a look at what's going on under St George's Hall. It's the gangs of girls on the Merseyrail asking you where you're going and where your missus got her shoes from, 'cos der lovely'. It's people who can just make you laugh, not with some prearranged routine, just by being themselves. That's what makes the place what it is. It's a city of full-on social interaction, whether it be narky, jokey, or just passing the time of day.

I come from the suburbs. In London it'd be High Barnet, especially since my little bit of suburbia is on the Northern Line too – though this is the Merseyrail we're talking about. Ever since I was a kid, the big place at the bottom of the hill has pulled me towards it. The city gave me two local football teams (I chose the ones in red), an accent I dub 'estuary Scouse' and the feeling that any number of possibilities were just a short bus or train ride away. Even now when I come back into town and walk down Dale St I feel like I'm on holiday, such is the power of its stunning architecture. Liverpool's not that big, the weather is at best changeable and at times it can be its own worst enemy – and yet, on a bright, sunny day in May with blinding girls thronging the streets, their sandpaper accents and Hollywood tans bewitching my senses, it feels like the most alive place on earth. I drink it in.

2008

Liverpool life …
When it all comes down

Mickey, written by Nicky Allt

❧

Mickey's story is the first Liverpool 'day in the life' take. My own will end this book. A good mate who didn't want his full name in print, I can respect that, even though I don't understand his insistence. A feller with local music in his bones, and proud of his city, a more dignified man you couldn't meet. Anyway Mickey lad, I don't think you'll begrudge me saying that much about you… eh… Mr Wonderful, Wonderful life?

Michael's fave band – Icicle Works, then Ian McNabb
Fave Liverpool song – at the moment – 'HMS Fable' by Shack
Fave book: Nicky's Boys from the Mersey. *Ah, thanks Mickey lad.*
TV Drama: Boys from the Blackstuff.
A Saturday afternoon bet. A drink at the Slaughterhouse. Fish and chips from the Lobster Pot. Then home for Match of the Day. Simple, but simple is best.

My head, banging and aching, felt mushy at the same time; like someone thumping away at Ringo's drum kit with a slush of old banana skins inside. Sunday morning hangovers eh! The thousandth in an erratically, wayward lifetime – part of me now – part of most who tread the expendable site labourers' ladder. Been battling with this stupid Chinese flu bug for weeks, my new excuse for getting drunk, you know, like a serious bender might pierce its sludge-like blockage. Not that I need an excuse! Think it bopped it till Chicken Fu Yung at three in the morning blocked the downward tubes again, bringing it snuffling on in. Kidding myself big time there though – about the alcohol curer – but, suppose its half-alright kidding yourself when you really need to.

The kids will be running around the house searching for their iPod this morning while my sister baby-sits and I once again take the building site trek for wages. I've been looking for months now. Even joined the people's pool the other day. People's pool is an employment agency where you leave your name and number till they phone you with an on-site start. If you ask me, might as well throw me and me name in a swimming pool for all that's worth. Anyway, with a walk ahead of me, a bit of a problem to bounce around with and a gunge-ridden skull cap thought music might work as a soother. I shouldn't really say a bit of a problem; a serious problem sounds more like it. God knows where I'm heading though... but, I've got to walk. Walk it off.

Couch-potato lazy today, aren't we, aren't we though – all of us. Thing is, if I don't get this squared off my life's not worth a one-legged Pierhead pigeon. Where to start? Here at the Mersey waterfront on the Sunday of the Mathew Street festival seems as good a place as any. See, clocking the big metal bird on top of the Liver building, it's swaying, reminding me of McCarthy and his two-bob, drug-dealing brother, Yoda. Germolene Yoda his many detractors call him. Ha! Twat of a name! Ugly little Yoda lookalike threateningly sways when he speaks to you, like a jealous nightclub drunk wanting to lamp you because you're walking through the exit doors linking the girl he tried to sweet talk earlier on. Always the evil leprechaun parked with Big Truck wanting to steal it on you or some other unfortunate, isn't it – the Joe Pesci of the gang. Straight out of the Star Wars bar with that skin – the stinking little toe-rag! Yoda got his name from spending all his drug dough trying to ride bareback with half-asleep crackhead whores and smackhead bores, before apparently rubbing Germolene down the old Japs-eye to kill off any impending disease. Mad eh? I know. Seems the fool with the drip-dry tool forgot to apply the stuff to his sandpapered face!

The whole of the Liver building is swaying now. I'll have to go for a flat out Dock Road waltz. Walk the ale off; walk the problem out. The wind keeps taking little bites out of me like piranhas jumping from the Mersey to rag at me cheekbones – over the landing stage, into your Adidas coat hood. No piranhas in this river though, just a fleet of moody, brown subs, funeral ashes aplenty and a trillion fucked-up dreams. Still fasten me hood tight though. Definitely need a soother this morning. Bit of Ian McNabb should settle the pumping vein. Feels like a wriggling worm at the side of me skull. 'When it all comes down' seeps into me, its driving beat battling with the thumping headache. Two Aspirin should even things up.

Ahead, a similar battle takes place as old sandstone history-makers battle with new glass-fronted mirror blocks. McCarthy owns a couple of apartments in there. And the footballer, Michael Owen, is supposed to own a couple higher up. A small, goal-scoring Welsh landlord playing for England, with a large sterling bank balance and a mansion based in Wales. That's culture for you eh! It's one of the problems today, isn't it, people owning three, four and twenty-five abodes, pushing up prices till they're higher than the Liverbird with nowhere left to push. A good pension they say or, in McCarthy's case, a good place for a laundering landlord to venture his dirty cabbage. Don't think Michael Owen would like to live next door to him or Yoda though.

I had a decent start down here two years ago, converting one of these older buildings into expensive modern apartments for the city's new breed. Unlike the last wave of immigrants, they never arrived via the legendary riverfront. The Chinese, Somalis, Nigerians, the Italians, even the Welsh and overwhelming Irish, these poor huddled masses all had their Liverpool Popeye day. This waterfront once played the role of Britain's own Ellis Island, as nine million people got siphoned in as potential Scousers before walking its entrance gangplank hoping to find greener grass on the banks of the Mersey; or, in the main, by using this Liverpool landing stage as a stepping stone to the new worlds of Australia, the Americas or New Zealand. One characteristic those fighting Irish definitely left behind is a hankering for a song.

Me, I can't go anywhere without a soundtrack. As Ian McNabb tells me that 'Love is all that matters, when it all comes down', that feeling of Sunday melancholia gets me thinking about the buildings and imprints of my past that are all coming down as part of this 'Big Dig' culture drive. The sun peek-a-booing its way round a dense, grey cloud means the feeling doesn't linger, as a neon stairway to heaven forcefully slices through. McNabb's giving me moments of optimism again. Clocking the beautiful Three Graces, I'm thinking, *yeah, this city is gonna look good but a lot more starched when the phoney culture dust settles.*

See, no melodramatic yearnings for the past aboard my ship, it's just, like most locals, I wish I had more of a *say* and more of a *do* in what's happening now and next. Once this Capital thing kicked in I thought my unemployment days were Ainsdale to Adelaide behind me. Eking a living throughout my early employment years, not in a life of Paddy Fagans did I think I'd see this city boom as it does presently. It may not be thunderous as Clapham Junction or some other London thoroughfares, but compared to Liverpool's and my own dole role in the big, bad 80s and early 90s, it's not like we've turned the corner, more we've jumped aboard a Porsche Cayenne for the Better City Marathon. Yeah, fast and more robust as a city, but for its populace, most of whom are not part of the new equation, I wonder if *their culture*, for which the city became *capital*, is theirs... really theirs? And, if it is, then why aren't the high-flying jobs that came steaming in on the gravy train being given to locals. 'Nobody qualified enough' the high-flying rubber stampers say. Not qualified at what – at living a Liverpool life? Culture – my arse – as one famously sponge-nosed local put it.

Walk the outer circumference of the inner-city Big Dig and ask locals what 'the culture thingy' means to them and you may be in for a roller coaster of a response. It's like one well-known clergyman put it: 'Tell them that good news is on its way, and they'll inform you: "Ah, its all pie in the sky, your grace, nothing will change for us, it'll never happen". Tell them the worst, life-threatening bad news and they'll say, "Ah, don't worry, it'll all be okay".' Well, bless me father, but they could be forgiven for saying 'Told you so' with the good news. To impact long term on any community you need movers and shakers who will be participants in new schemes and ideas for the foreseeable. Not suits who ride in on the first government cash-rattlers, only to ride straight back out in the first grant-mobiles to hit some other town or city. In and out idea makers we've seen aplenty. Now idea stayers and doers... well, that'd be using a bit too much foresight wouldn't it?

Along with my struggle to work locally came a problem many ordinary people have to deal with today. Thing is, most of them wouldn't have dealt with it in the way that I did. Let me explain. Living in a quiet, suburban street with young children the sudden breakdown in law and order, fitting to most liberalized British cities today, arrived the moment Biddy McCarthy, his brother Yoda and the rest of their scabby-arsed clan moved in. Then along came the cling-on gang, people's fear, then the drugs, followed by seven or eight years of almost utter lawlessness. Good people move out, bad people move in; yeah, yeah, usual story...

Till one evening I'm at the front window of my humble drum, seeing as the noise from the mass gathering has reached Motorhead at Glastonbury proportions. Catching my face at the window, some of the young guns, preening for the young handbags, started openly mocking me. Now curtain peeping has never been my idea of a decent way of passing time, more indecently living your life watching other people living, but those red curtains and mocking faces were my rag-to-a-bull

– my baying crowd. Getting caught at the drapes, and worse, being mocked for it, meant I'd lowered myself to the indecent suburban habits of Mr and Mrs Curtain Peep. And believe me nobody hated those knobhead nosey neighbours more than me.

Straight out the front door, I confronted the mouthiest of the bunch. He seemed shocked that Mr Curtain Peep should be up-in-his-face without hesitation in front of his black watch, death-hooded amigos. Heated words became heated gestures as the lid-with-the-grid started to bob, weave and sway like he was about to launch the big right-hander. Sick to death of watching my step, outside my own front step, I ultimately flipped. A fighter's youth had taught me the basics of putting your weight behind a decent right cross, but, as he danced at nipple height the left hook I caught him with shocked not only him, it jaw-dropped me and the rest of the crew. It was as though the left hook ghost of Liverpool stadium had blown directly through me to land bang on the lid's grid. Lights out, he was star gazing a-bo-bos.

Though I didn't know it at the time it was Biddy's younger kidder, Yoda. Other young guns backed off, while the young handbags stood aghast all tango-faced and lip-twisted. Knowing I'd overstepped the mark and that I had to back up the killer hook had me randomly barking orders. 'Now don't bother coming near this house anymore!' And the obvious, 'Let that be a warning!' seemed to have the desired effect as the gang dragged mouthpiece and themselves out of reach. Only when distanced did one of them turn and shout about how I'd regret my action. Hooded shithouses!

A sleepless night on the couch, expecting a police knock or worse, turned into a sleepless week of expecting the worst. Nothing happened. An uneasy peace brought two speeding tickets that week, the week the culture tag was won, from the same candidly-robbing-you yellow camera that bled motorists on the main road near my home. Putting the driving penalties down to nervy uneasiness, some might put the 36mph and 38mph I was driving at down to government-sponsored highway robbery.

A week or two passed before I received a messy threatening letter calling me an 'arl lunatic' (38 at the time), stating I'd be sorry for my recent lights-out performance. Cutting to the sprint: another letter arrived, the mob returned, I chased two of them who were pissing on my front wall with a baseball bat, only to be ambushed by a gang of about twenty. Swiping out, I caught two of them well enough to crack calcium, was duly charged by them and their hard-done parents, and

ended up in Walton prison for three months – it really was that quick.
Expecting one of Biddy's boys to come a-calling in jug, they never did.
I found out rather quickly that he had more enemies than friends, and I
was jail embraced by some of the hardest hitters you could wish to meet.
I needed that inside, though it still shocked me. Some people reckoned
I needed a medal and congratulations, but no street or prison glory
was ever going to pay my mortgage. While in jug I read every book I
could on local history. St Nicholas's church, standing here in front of
me – the seaman's church – played a large part in that hometown study.
Below its walls machinery and workers build away, oblivious of me and
the fact it's Sunday. I can hear the drill over the sound of Ian McNabb's
early band, the Icicle Works. Taking the headphones off, it's time to
enquire about a start.

'Hiya mate; who's the boss round here?'

'It's fella with tash; him over there.'

Detecting a Lancashire twang I don't hold much hope, but like I
was saying this Liverpool culture started at this waterfront, so it's as
good a place as any. Reaching the yellow hard hat of the foreman he
can't see or hear me. Waving a hand in front of his face, he turns, taking
his mufflers off. My question, the obvious 'any work for a builder's
labourer on here mate?' makes me feel like the new millennium Yozzer
Hughes.

'You've got to go through agency mate.'

'Oh yeah, and where's that then?'

'It's over in Manchester.'

'You got the number there?'

Being slightly aggressive in tone gets him respectful as he fum-
bles for a pen and paper to jot down an 0161 number; probably the
Manchester people's pool. You have to construct sentences with a little
aggression on a building site – act Johnny-Concrete tough – otherwise you might not look up for the job. Co-workers eye me warily. I
thank him. Traipsing off site, the dingy Atlantic Tower Hotel throws
ugly 1970s shadows across Tithebarn Street. Looks like the Pierhead
seagulls have had the runs and shat all over it. I wouldn't want to be
part of any team building another one of those diarrhoea-coloured
eyesores. Walking towards Old Hall Street I dip into Exchange Flags
and feel its silence. Once thronged with merchants buying and selling
commodities, it feels ghostly with only a lone tourist taking snapshots
of Admiral Nelson's statue. A hero to the merchants, the Admiral's
victories allowed them to ply their trade freely to the rest of the world.

Thinking about freedom gained – even the Nelson type – what type of freedom do we have when a local man can't get work during a boom time in his hometown? And, who gives a sailor's sod?

Fancy-looking yellow Culture pamphlets lie disregarded at the foot of the monument. Turning the page it boldly states the date the tag was won, like the date has become monumental itself. '8.10 am Wednesday, 4 June, 2003. The future of Liverpool changed forever. Sunny, probably not a cloud in the sky, and then a plane circled the city of Liverpool with a banner: We won it!' The pamphlet – tarted up – wears a suit and tie like the people who cheered the loudest. Now don't get me boxed-off as cynical Sidney, but when the likes of your Robyn Archers come waltzing in Matilda-style from the land of koalas and kangaroos to organize my city's cultural celebration – on top-whack wages – while I struggle to get an on-site start, then you'll understand me when I refer to it as a bit of cock-eyed culture. And no sooner had she waltzed in Qantas quality class and waltzed back out again than I got to thinking about her flights, earnings and keep while McCarthy and Yoda were trying to make my life a misery. Another piece of cock-eyed culture reared up at me when those two had the temerity to offer me security work once they found I'd been embraced by their enemies. You know, like they can buy absolutely anyone.

Local newspapers have been inundated with complaint letters about the disparity in handing out Culture work, Culture jobs and Culture money to non-local based firms and workers. Most of them note how as they travel the city they see the amount of non-Liverpool based companies 'parked-up and doing the work' while they struggle to even reach the bidding stage. Patrick McKibbin from Kirkdale wrote one such letter proclaiming: *I am writing to say how disgusted I am in this so-called Capital of Culture. We are family-run small, mastic asphalt company who try to get work from our local councils but it continues to fall on deaf ears. I feel so annoyed when driving around Norris Green, Croxteth, Kirkdale and Kirkby and see mastic asphalt firms from Wigan, Manchester, Bolton and Chorley working on council houses and property in Liverpool. I feel so let down seeing these contractors as we don't get a look in. What an outcry there would be if outside contractors came in and did work for their local councils. It would just not happen, so why should it happen to a Liverpool-based company trying to get some work from our own councils?* It's a headache that seems to be growing instead of decreasing. Mr McKibbin, it's like I hear your asphalt wagon drive by as I speak.

Thankfully this headache seems to be easing now, with an

Anadin attack drowning the last remnants of a throbbing vein and Shack sending it overboard on the HMS Fable. A Liverpool band of fable, the Head brothers get into my head with melodic ease as the nondescript backside of the Town Hall looms. The Lord Mayor's first-floor view overlooking Castle Street has to be one of the finest sights in the downtown area. Even when the city's economy and standing got well and truly ravaged mid-eighties, and it looked to the populace like Thatcher and her cronies were hoping to kill it off before dancing upon its grave, this street always bloomed and boomed. It seemed a part of Liverpool that would and could never die. One day, in the not-too-distant, maybe I shall dance upon her grave and happily get carted to the nearest Bridewell in the process. God, I've got to let go. It's almost twenty years on and I still hate that fucking nervous breakdown gob of hers!

Such is a child's imagination that as a young pup, sat upon my father's shoulders to witness Bill Shankly raise the 1965 FA Cup in victory, the tumultuous roar that followed as the team were welcomed onto the Lord Mayor's balcony had me thinking that the foundations were about to crumble and wash my beloved team into the Mersey. Outside is a scaffold and sign belonging to McCarthy's firm. As he diversifies and launders into legal society, feeling as I do, I want to rip it down, throw it aside and sabotage the job in progress. It's one of those days. The team and the city never floated off down the Mersey estuary to the welcoming Irish Sea, like that 'economically viable cabinet' would've loved and hoped some twenty years later. Now, as I stand here in the throes of city resurgence and regeneration, clocking McCarthy's scaffold, I wonder if it's viable to think that my marriage has a fighting chance.

See, starting work down in Shropshire, with the mortgage getting attended to, my wife, as an excuse for an affair, reckoned that her feelings, emotions and needs were not being attended to. Ha, I mean, you have to laugh. Sometimes it's like they want you to make money but don't want you to go out and get it. Well, we can't all sit in the garage with our old John Bull printing sets and become master forgers. When I met her she was the life and soul, loving a party and loving the attention. Looking about, unemployment, hardship and redundancy were rife. Although economic misery spread right across the board and the consequences of the London government did more damage politically and internally to Liverpool than the German Luftwaffe had managed in the Second World War, it seemed we were all in it together: for better, for worse. Riots were rioted, marches were marched and picket lines were picketed. Now it's all, *you've either got it or you haven't*, with people questioning your worth in pounds, pence and pricey pullovers, not in person. It's like the home-owning sons and daughters of little Maggie Mortgage are all fully grown and greed is healthy, money is god and equity is everyone's middle name.

Anyway, back in the day – sorry – my hardship days – you fought on, met a girl, had children, made a nest, foraged for food, and made a life as best you could. And working away was how I got through most of the above and made the most. Working away put food on the table while my music kept me sane and filled in a lot of lonely bedsit hours without loved ones for company. While she never had my company, during my latest bout of working away, I came home one weekend to find she'd been seen out and about with McCarthy.

Now Liverpool's a village concerning Chinese whispers, sightings and conspiracy theories, but when I tugged her to find out if it was true she basically spilled the beans first take. No lies, no fucking about, just a bang-on between the eyes, yes! She was always a good-looker Marie, but fool that I am I never thought she'd embarrass me or the kids in that way. After a month or so of having a drug-dealer's mattress tied to her back, without ever finding the big stash underneath, he eventually tired of her and she came running back to the building site fool. Will it work out? Can't really say at the moment, but I'm a doubting Thomas who got used to having a Thomas the Tank, put it that way. Once again the long, dark nights, this time at home, were filled with music as a comforter and thoughts of my children's futures. Where would I be without them both?

On a lighter note, one of the reasons I keep mentioning music is they recently pulled the plug on the city's Mathew Street music festival, and walking the ale off and looking for graft apart, it's the other reason why I'm down here early Sunday morning. Though traffic-free early, the streets don't feel the same without the set-up of the outdoor stages, yet Culture Company chief executive, Jason Harborow, reckons he was 'happy' with the decision to pull the plug on the best weekend in the Liverpool calendar year. He and 'them', whoever they are, had 'independent' advice from a safety consultant company called Capita, who made it very clear that the event was not safe in its current format… blah-de-blah-de-blah. The old health and safety blag eh. Could be a massive shortfall in funds just weeks prior to the festival weekend had something to do with it… hmm? Ten years in the making, the festival's overnight plug-pulling was a sick joke, and an 800-year-old sick joke at that. Councillor Paul Clein said: 'Heads should roll at the highest level'. We as Liverpool people openly laugh and say: 'But will they fuck!'

For me to tell you my thoughts on the culture thingy, my hatred of McCarthy's bloodsucking mob and my love of music and my city, I have to paint you a little characterization, and seeing as it's scrolled on this wall that the Bunnymen are back and Ian McCulloch is God, let me character things up a little by starting with those brilliant Eric's upstarts. Early eighties I was a big Echo and the Bunnymen fan, till some of the darker songs reminded me of how dark my own life was at the time. Offered a start on an East London building site I had no option. Cash in hand being order of the day meant my mate could carry on signing-on at Walton Job Centre while I made the most of shitty digs in Bayswater. Weekday settled in London, we fast acquired our own little crew. One big-city night, jumping the Tube into the West End to see the Bunnymen play, a young East End gangster wannabe one of the Scouse bricklayers on site had gotten friendly with tagged along...

He'd been knocking about the local Bayswater pubs and drinking in our company for a short while prior. Knowing how scarce jobs and money were in the North, Wannabe (it became his name) boldly mentions he and a Canning Town acquaintance might be looking for cocaine carriers – mules, or mugs, to carry and make delivery to Liverpool once a month. Seeing as the Friday train out of Euston had become a party on wheels (the ale on the rail), packed from wheel to luggage compartment like an Bombay cattle train, our mate the brick-layer, supplementing his fifty-pound-a-day income (after a couple of years of unemployment, playing catch-up he called it) starts humping a large bag of the white stuff alongside his spirit level and trowel. And I mean a *large* bag. Few months into the wheeling, dealing, drinking friendship and the same bricklayer's got a rampant Charlie addiction, an every night, except for Wednesdays for some unknown reason, drinking habit and a various group of Liverpool builders fed up with his unreliability and his dirt-dealing ways. Bugling being Scouse slang for snorting cocaine he's quickly labelled the Bugling Bricklayer.

Friday comes, Friday goes, till one fine afternoon in July, with everyone ensconced in the smothering glow of the ale on the rail, and Jonesie the Bricklayer bugling for England, the bizzies jumped aboard at Crewe under the pretence that too much ale had been drunk and too loud a commotion was being made aboard the five o'clock rattler. Apparently passenger complaints had been blown through to Transport Police by the frustrated on-board clippy who couldn't pass through, leaving him unable to clip for the trip. The boarding uniforms ordered everyone to be seated for the remaining forty-five-minute journey to Liverpool's Lime Street Station. Problem being: crowded migrant workers' train meant not enough seats. Most of the workers, returning home for the weekend to see loved ones, thought it their right to carry on drinking after a hard week's graft away from family familiarity. The transport cops, keeping an uneasy peace all the way to the first sniff of the Mersey, remained cool, calm and collected.

Arriving at the platform, early evening sun shot neon beams of light through the huge Lime Street roof. Stepping from the train, our little crew, numbering six, including the powdered-up bricklayer, gets fully swooped on. Not by the watchful wardens of Crewe but by our own uniforms-in-waiting, Platform Plod. Some workers disembarking the train assumed we were being lifted due to excessive drinking, or somebody had said something way-off the orderly radar. Roughly ten coppers frog-marched the six of us through the busy gate to an interview room within the station. In transit the Jones boy starts trailing site dust from his clothing with the amount of twitching he's doing. Making out he needed to speak to his waiting wife he went to walk off, before Sergeant Muscles unceremoniously dragged him back by the dusty collar. Through the drink and haze some lads had forgotten about Jonesie's new snorting sideline. Desperate to be rid of the bag, the cops eyed him suspiciously. Not being in possession, we all walked upright and dispassionate. Carrying, he jitterbugged off the train and did the twist through the station.

Once all bags were placed on the floor of the interview room and questions were asked and happily answered by all except one, the police thought it a good idea to have a quick check of the holdalls before we were each dismissed back to our own humble-drums. A spotty-faced, young-arse copper, looking more YTS school-leaver than Officer Probe-the-Globe, started asking whose bag belonged to whom. People naturally reached for their own tool-laden bag, till there was Jonesie and the lonesome holdall. YTS, assuming it was his, asked why he hadn't picked it up. Replying in blubbering whisky speak, the drunken act began in earnest.

Spending the whole weekend in holding cells we were eventually released with the Jones boy still insisting he had no idea how the package found its way inside his bag of tools. Unexpectedly, on my behalf, it became local headline news. Suddenly gangs of Liverpool building workers were under suspicion for supposedly being involved in the transportation of illegal drugs. Of course, it was utter media bullshit – a story to run with! If Jonesie was one of the first drug-dealing bricklayers to get a three-year sentence, then I can assure you he was one of very few. With London and the south coast being inundated with thousands of migrant Liverpool building workers he was the fool-mule exception. Once the story hit the newsstands and names were named and those Liverpool lullabies were passed around, then family shame and mud started to stick where it shouldn't. It did my head in! While Jonesie got used to not having to build walls – the ones at Walton jail were way high enough – I continued to work away in London and found out through more Liverpool lullabies that London Wannabe was delivering his gear to one of McCarthy's associates – another bugling bricky with small-time Escobar intentions. He duly ended up brown bread a few years later. People on the street find these things out early, the bizzies usually find out way too late.

Jonesie wrote frequently to most of us while in prison – suppose he was suffering from 'off the Charlie' cell paranoia and those 'need a friend blues' while inside. An excellent bricklayer, he hit the drug scene again… and again; addicted to the fast money he told me. Well, you can have all the snazzy motors, lavish holidays and natty designer togs this side of the Empire State building, but no fast million or two could compensate me for an eight stretch inside some grotty Northern prison, two'ed up with a fat, greasy-palmed, four-eyed Liberace from Huddersfield. During his last five-year snooze in Durham prison he wrote me this poem. Though roughly written and not the greatest literary piece to emanate from inside the slammer walls, it still tells the story of how a lack of opportunity or unemployment can lead to the devil finds work for idle hands and empty pockets. It was the last I heard from him.

Soulless

A kid I knew once asked of me
'What do you do to climb the tree?'
To dig your way out of this hole?
A few quid more without selling your soul?

You need a job where jobs are scarce
To drop some dough in your Ma's purse
Find a stash, your pot of gold
Find the answer without selling your soul

Temptation rears its ugly head
To jump into the Devil's bed
All your people are on the dole
They dangle carrots to sell your soul

A college course, and then a scheme
While other cats have got the cream
You want to live before you're old
It's tempting not to sell your soul

You pack your bags you're on your way
Down the smoke where people pay
You leave your Ma, your kin, your fold
On the road to selling your soul

Grafting on sites, finally in collar
Eight days a week to earn top dollar
Living in digs is taking its toll
Then someone offers to sell your soul

Clocking the movers, I want more dough
A car, a house, the way to go
Soon I've cheated and lied and stole
It catches up this selling your soul

Ten years on since I left school
Nobody's toe-rag, nobody's fool
I'm thinking I've dug my way out of the hole
Laying the brick to not selling your soul

It's Maggie's England, I'm out on the town
An acquaintance asks if I'm fooling around
'You earn crap money, want some gold?'
'Carry some gear and sell your soul?'

Earning big, being a mule
Transporting drugs, being his fool
Soon got my own mules to carry my gold
The absolute point of selling my soul

Feeding the weak, poison and shit
This is where I made my bit
I'm killing my own, I've chosen my role
I'm driving a Merc I've sold my soul

Tebbit had said, 'Get on your bike'
And you can go as far as you like
Well I have gone as far as I can go
Empty as fuck, I've sold my soul

So about this kid who asked of me
'What do you do to climb the tree?'
He's now dead, he'll never grow old
That kid was me, I've sold my soul.

Jonesie, December 1994

High unemployment in the Liverpool area no doubt led to a surge in crime as people searched for their next crust. Once people found illegal ways of finding that crust and realized it could be found on a more regular basis than solid employment, then some career workers became career criminals, with the Conservative party happy to stand by and let it ferment. It makes things all the more laughable when today's Tory leader David Cameron refers to his cronies as the party of law and order. I have to give at least thirteen ha ha's to that! Short memories most politicians, maybe brought on by a lack of milk vitamins in their growing years in this case.

As career criminals got into heavier criminality and unemployment remained stagnant and a long, long way above the national average, a major place to wash dirty money was Liverpool city centre – the local 'sterling launderette'. Private investment in bars, shops and restaurants ran alongside European status-one funding money, awarded to the city as economic 'hand-out' aid. And the daft thing is, top launderers like McCarthy were given more money to help their businesses grow, adding legal aid to the huge flow of illegal lemonade already flowing in a speedy stream to the expanding pool under the king-size mattress.

Back of the Town Hall, Exchange Flags, where I'm stood now, was a place where people came to 'exchange things', to barter goods for goods. It seems strange that as I scan the place, feeling an eerie emptiness of history swirling about me, I too have swapped an old hankering for employment away from redundancy central for a hankering for employment within the regenerated walls of the Capital of Culture. Plenty of work I'm told, but not for me. Cranes dotted about the landscape usually suggest abundant construction work; cranes planted all over the show, a serious building boom, but it's definitely not boom time for Mickey Mac.

In the history of *my* city there can't have been any bigger building booms than the one happening at this moment in time. The regeneration that Liverpool is going through, allied to its 800th birthday celebration and the Culture title, makes me feel like I can't contribute, I'm not on the guest list and that the title has nothing to do with me as a Mersey citizen: a Scouser. And while I struggle to make ends meet and find a job, then notice McCarthy's company signs planted about the place, well... put it this way, I watched Adam Sandler and Jack Nicholson's *Anger Management* comedy movie three times last week and it didn't help. For those proud Scousers like me who want to play a part in the 'goings on' it feels like someone has put signs up on the main arterial roads into the city, like Edge Lane, Scotland Road and Aigburth Road, stating 'No access', 'Keep out', 'Private function till further notice'.

It's seems strange that at a time when opportunities to shape the face of Liverpool have sizeably increased, they remain limited for the vast majority of its people. Me, I'm fucking annoyed! End of! The musical gigs I'm supposed to be meeting a few mates at later – Europe's biggest free festival by the way – will all be taking place indoors, and the bottom line is, that's where all the major issues concerning my city take place, with myself and all its citizens locked outside misting up the glass panels. It's the old 'poor kids staring into the toy shop window at Christmas' routine – new millennium style.

In truth, it's not just the multitudes being left out on the pavement – even high-profile actors like Liverpool's own Ian Hart was quoted as saying: 'The thing that kept nagging away at me was what has the Capital of Culture money been spent on? I'd be speaking to mates of mine and they'd be telling me about good ideas they'd put forward to the Culture Company which had been knocked back. So I thought it'd be a good idea to produce a documentary following the money trail from the moment when Liverpool was first awarded Capital of Culture. You know, these are the people who thought it'd be a good idea to put an Australian who had never been in the city before in charge, and she quit after eight months taking her big salary with her. So, I'd like to look at making a documentary on that.' And Ian, so would we mate, believe me, so would we.

The Culture Company, just four months short of Culture year, have just had to go cap-in-hand to the government through the city's Liberal council for a twenty million pound loan to pay for next year's celebrations. So yeah, Ian, we'd like you to make that documentary right away squire. Labour leader and opposition to the Liberals, councillor Joe Anderson, condemned the situation as a major catastrophe and said the Liberal council should have been honest with the people from the start about how we were going to pay for Culture year. The cap-in-hand move was instantly turned away by Treasury officials who said Liverpool would have to pay for the celebration itself seeing as it was a one-off. And how were the council going to pay the loan back, if given? Over five years with cash raised from additional 1% council tax rises. Yeah, the multitudes left outside on the pavement would have to stump up the loan money once again… Un-fucking-believable!

The MIS (Men in Suits) spent a heap of money chasing around after Will Alsop's 'Cloud building' dream, and on Robyn Archer's two years on the Culture board, when she in fact spent less than four months in Liverpool while booking some expensive dance troupes who no one was interested in seeing. It's a never-ending joke. One day the penny will drop that Liverpool is a unique place full of proudly pushy people who would willingly work themselves to the bone to get things right for half the money these idiots throw around. Ah, I'm sick of it. I've heard about sounding like a stuck record but the bringing in of outside charlatans and Machiavellian company men is like having to listen to Jive Bunny jive-arsing you non-stop for fifty years about 'that's just the way it is'.

As I wander down Castle Street, gazing upon beautiful architecture, the Head brothers sing about the streets of Kenny and I wonder if anyone from that vast sprawl of terraced streets in North Liverpool has been asked about their views on Culture year, or if one person, just one person from the thousands who live there has ever had a sniff of a culture job. They are, after all, 'the culture'. No jive-arsing from Shack just pure headache-soothing melodies.

Another building site shows face. Its vans, wagons and machinery show alien numbers once more. I go to walk in. Two Irish accents change my mind. The Irishmen in conversation clock me like I'm the alien in my hometown. Without asking I can tell it's a closed shop. Turning to walk away I'm thinking of cold-hearted McCarthy and his lowlife brother, Yoda, and whether they'll ever make a move on me like Biddy already has on my frozen-hearted missus. Then I'm thinking of her and her statement about searching for a new and more glamorous lifestyle, and of my newly regenerated, polished-up city and no work, which gives me the reasoning, 'fuck it! I'm going for a bevvy'. Where's the Crocodile boozer or the Grapes or Ma Egerton's... somewhere un-starched and left alone.

These Irish workers, County Mayo boys (wearing Mayo badges) must think I'm a strange one, roving about down here on a Sunday morning with my head in a morning-after cloud. The alien, goose-pimply feeling that overwhelms me is countered only by Shack's fine melodies which bring me back to the here and now and get me questioning the drink option. I know it's not the best one but, like I've said, sometimes you need to kid yourself, even if it's only for a short while. Like I've also told you, without the music of my city... well, at this place in time, with everything supposedly on the up, I'd be acting the Mickey Oddball by being on a permanent downer. My Liverpool eh... my Mersey culture... my alien feeling... my saving grace... Bevvy it is...

~   ~   ~

Just an hour later footnote... Well, that pumping vein at the side of my head has wriggled somewhere else now – thank God – but when it all comes down to the larger headache of where my life's going, where I'm going to get work and whether or not I'll ever get back with the missus, or even if I want to, they remain personal issues that I'll have to sort. And yeah, I know I'm drinking too much lately but it's not an illness or anything, it's just sometimes... you know. Thing is, I'd just love to give a helping hand to sorting this city's future, because deep in my guts I feel that given the chance to do something positive in the place where my heart lies would go a long way in helping me deal with those personal issues sooner rather than later, and in the positive sense I need to move forward... fast forward, in this newly starched city of ours – welcome to the new Liverpool... 2008 style.

Summer 2007

Political life ...
The Regeneration Professionals

Peter Furmedge

❊

*I asked Peter Furmedge if he would write a political viewpoint for the book
and about 2008. Having worked in a range of regeneration jobs and in a
host of voluntary positions for that sector, Peter has represented the North
Liverpool community on an array of panels and committees, and, where he
said, 'all the big money gets carved up'. So, I state categorically that I am quite
proud to have his declarations and opinions here in print. I make no bones
about the fact that not only is he more qualified than myself to do so, but he is
arguably the finest political observer we have in this city. I've been egging him
on to write his own book; hopefully he will do so real soon...*

That one obvious appointment, that of Phil Redmond to the position of vice-chair of the Liverpool Culture Company, appears
to have lifted the sense of gloom enveloping the build-up to
Liverpool's year as European Capital of Culture is enough to show that,
far from being ultra-critical, over-demanding archetypal 'whinging
Scousers', the people of the city didn't really expect much from 2008
– just not to be taken for mugs by those taking a ride on the latest
carriage to be hitched onto the gravy train to Lime Street. Since the city
of Liverpool was colonized by a cadre of regeneration 'professionals'
in the wake of the 1981 Liverpool 8 uprising, the locals have grown
used to a succession of suits and generic middle England accents being
paraded as saviours of the inner city. Once the Militant-led Labour
council was safely out of the way, Heseltine's Toxteth-Task-Force-
inspired trickle of 'regenerators' became a flood, a deluge that has
irreversibly changed the city's local government mindset. While mildly
annoying for those who've had to deal with the post-Militant careerist
influx, the majority of Liverpudlians were prepared to just make their
own way and blank out the pillage of the city taking place in the upper
echelons. Generation after generation of 'regeneration professionals'

have followed in Heseltine's wake and yet the city remains home to some of Britain's most deprived neighbourhoods.

In the summer of 2007, however, the slumbering masses were eventually shaken out of their relative indifference to the city being used as some sort of right of passage for apprentice bureaucrats and the aspiring political class. The Liverpool Culture boffins, who must have thought they'd been operating in some sort of fireproof bubble given the ease with which they had been allowed to escape public rebuke to this point, had failed in their most basic task: organizing a piss-up in Liverpool. Failure after failure, extravagant misallocation of funds and the exclusion of all but an elite circle had passed by with little more than a 'What would you expect anyway?' from the man or women on the street. Then the Mathew Street festival was cancelled. Liverpool's traditional bank holiday party, the biggest free music festival in Europe, an event that was central to the city's original pitch for Capital of Culture status, ditched by previously faceless officials without any recourse to the elected councillors to whom they are allegedly accountable, and who in turn answer to us at the largely ignored local elections.

Cancelling the Mathew Street festival brought the very existence of the Liverpool Culture Company to the fore of local consciousness. People who'd thought the whole fiasco was the 100 per cent fault of the council were suddenly made aware that 100 people were being paid an average of forty grand a year to deliver the city's culture programme, with the big cheese 'earning' £140,000. All this in a city where average household income only just tops the £20,000 mark, and typical of the so-called partnership approach that has removed any semblance of democracy and accountability from the running of the city's key initiatives. How do you get on the Culture Company Board? By standing in elections? By appointment? By invitation? More to the point, how can the people of Liverpool get anybody off it? The erstwhile chairman of the Liverpool Culture Company, Drummond Bone of Liverpool University, once announced that although he was leaving the University he would continue to head the Culture Board. How? Surely his only mandate was as representative of the University. And who decided that the University was entitled to a seat on the Board anyway?

But it's not only the Capital of Culture programme where a board operates at arm's length from the council, allocating public money via an array of self-serving, self-appointed and self-preserving boards and committees. Liverpool's application for Capital of Culture status claimed that by 2008 Everton would be playing at a 55,000 multi-purpose stadium at King's Dock. Who was to blame for the failure to deliver the King's Dock stadium and, equally to the point, who decided that its replacement would be a half-sized MEN arena? The council? Well sort of, but Liverpool Vision deal with that sort of thing. So, Liverpool Vision, what went wrong? Better see the landowners, English Partnerships or the Northwest Development Agency. Nothing to see over here, move on to Government Office Northwest. Arghh... I'm gonna blame Derek Hatton!

So, back to Mathew Street and whose fault was it really? The Culture Company? Well they didn't dig the roads up did they? That was the Big Dig and that's the council's job. So, Warren, whaddaya say? Please don't say to go back to Liverpool Vision, please, they'll only give me a brochure about the City Centre Movement Strategy and send me back to Government Office and I'll end up speaking to that crowd down at City Focus. So who ballsed this one up? All of them and none of them, and most of them are the same people! Confused?

With all the different agencies, quangos and committees you'd think there must be hundreds of different people involved. The reality is that most of the same people serve on multiple boards and panels, appointed from one to the other until they can't see where the line of accountability starts. It's a process that's replicated throughout the city, with local partnerships appointing people to a multitude of additional partnerships dealing with everything from childcare and youth clubs to the development of strategic investment areas. Everyone's responsible yet, at the same time, no one is particularly responsible for anything. Call the council, you're through to Liverpool Direct – part-owned by BT. Want to inquire about a plot of land or an empty building, then contact 20/20 – a 'joint venture' with Mouchel Parkman. Who's supposed to have spent the past seven years 'upgrading' the Dock Road and Edge Lane? That'll be the Liverpool Land Development Company and the 'local' Strategic Investment Area 'partnership'. The same arrangement that somehow managed to ensure that people in Gillmoss ended up living in nothing short of a war zone while the government money that was intended to enable them to move out went unspent.

Amid the confusion and disarray that's shrouded the city's build-up to 08, enter Phil Redmond and a sprinkling of Scouse stardust, albeit Scouse stardust hailing from the non-purple-binned environs of Frodsham. Macca's playing Anfield, Ringo's going to be drumming on the roof of St George's Hall, and all's apparently going well. The new-style slimmed down Culture Company Board can't undo the cancellation of the Mathew Street Festival, the sold-out but somehow loss-making Summer Pops or the Robyn Archer debacle. But the new approach does beg the question of why we needed to adopt the Billy Big Bollocks route in the first place. Capital of Culture isn't the Olympics. It isn't even the school sports day version of the Olympics that our east Lancastrian cousins ended up with. It's a place-marketing opportunity, a cherry to put on top of the Objective One icing on the regeneration cake. Capital of Culture is Liverpool's fifteen minutes of fame, the big chance to showcase 'the world in one city', or at the very least our aspiration to be the world in one city. It's the one big chance to put right the misconceptions of the place and the populace that were spawned by Thatcher's henchmen, and duly disseminated by their media yes-men, by unleashing the creative forces of the city on a sceptical world.

Instead, the arm's length Culture Company was formed and sure enough, just like many other new companies, the primary purpose of that company became... the promotion and survival of the company. What was the point of all that? The city has a package that needs sharpening up and promoting, not taking apart and replacing. The museums and galleries are already here, the sporting events have been taking care of themselves for over a century, two local fellers have built up a Beatles industry and a lad from Everton launched one of the most famous clubs in the world. The city has world-class writers in the likes of Jimmy McGovern and Alan Bleasdale, there are theatres that can host everything from amateur dramatics to the national opera, and the Royal Liverpool Philharmonic stands comparison with the best. The list goes on and on, highbrow to popular, from oratorios in the Anglican Cathedral to showcase nights at the Picket.

What was needed was an arm of the council dedicated to pulling all the strands of Liverpool culture together, assisting with fund raising and, most importantly, promoting the city and its offering like never before. What we didn't need was an entire organization taking strict control and trying to impose its definition of culture upon a city that has dissent written in its DNA. Culture doesn't have a strategy, it's organic and anarchistic and spontaneous. It doesn't need 'creative direction' from above; it needs the authorities to ensure that there is an environment in which creativity can flourish and where funding allocations recognize the value of investing in grass roots programmes. Four million pounds a year on wages alone, the Liverpool Culture Company's priorities are clear as daylight. One year's wage bill will dwarf the entire 'community programme' for 2008. In fact the combined 'Creative Communities' and 'Innovation and Development' grants programmes amount to just about ten average annual salaries in the 100-strong Culture Company. Rather than creating an environment that nurtures local culture, ensuring that young people have a genuine opportunity to 'buy into' what's great about the city, the Culture Company has spent, spent, spent like a municipally backed Viv Nicholson. From the mad (spending £200,000 just to find out that it's a stupid idea to try to drain a dock and put a concert in it) to the bad (hundreds of thousands of pounds paid to a member of staff who never actually worked in the UK, never mind the city of Liverpool). The company now faces a £20 million budget deficit – and the city awaits the intervention of the District Auditor and the subsequent surcharging and suspension from public office of those responsible. Well it doesn't, but it should.

As if it's not enough to be profligate with its own budget, the Culture Company has wasted no time in digging into everybody else's, aided and abetted by an overly compliant council. The subsidy given to the Summer Pops programme, which wasn't even held in Liverpool in 2007, has been well documented. The channelling of Neighbourhood Renewal Fund, meant to be spent on relieving deprivation in some of Britain's poorest wards, into the loss-making 08 Place Capital of Culture Shop in Whitechapel has been less well publicized. £1.4 million of Neighbourhood Renewal Fund, diverted from areas like Norris Green, Everton and Toxteth, was granted by the council towards the construction of the 08 Place. Given the Culture Company's projected community programme of £400,000, this £1.4 million represents a financial transfusion from Liverpool's most deprived neighbourhoods into a glorified One Stop Shop of some £1 million. Never mind though, you can still write a line for a poem or have pile of party hats and balloons for your street party. In spite of this spectacular level of subsidy, the Culture Company still projects annual losses of more than £500,000 per year from its city centre store!

No doubt the final figures will still show the 08 Place to have been a resounding success; but just how it will prove delivery of outcomes in Neighbourhood Renewal target areas is anyone's guess. In one respect the 08 Place 'project' is doomed to succeed; how can it fail to achieve its target visitor numbers when it has replaced the two existing tourist information centres, operated by the now sidelined Merseyside Tourism

Board, at Queen Square and Albert Dock? Displacement, as it's known in the doublespeak of regeneration, is nothing new to the Culture Company. They have assumed control of a number of successful events that predated the award of Capital of Culture for 2008, infamously abandoning the previously volunteer-led Mersey River Festival. There was a banner draped over the Churchill Way flyover during Liverpool FC's homecoming from their European Cup Final victory in Istanbul proclaiming that the event had been organized by the Liverpool Culture Company. Just how Shankly, Paisley, Dalglish and Joe Fagan (oh, OK then, and Catterick and Kendall) managed to parade around the city in open-top buses without the aid of a £4 million per annum workforce, only God knows.

The announcement that Capital of Culture was to be awarded to Liverpool in June 2003 signalled the launch of a series of themed years, Year of Faith, Year of the Sea, or some such thing, and so on, intended to take the city up to and beyond 2008. That nobody has a clue what the current year's theme is supposed to be is an indictment of the Culture Company's abject failure to deliver even the most basic component of its apparent role, that of marketing the programme and engaging local people. The degree of relief expressed by many upon hearing of the appointment of Phil Redmond as vice-chair (Creative Direction), and general front man for the ailing enterprise, was generated as much by finally seeing a familiar face at the helm as anything else. People now feel that they know who's running the show, even though the actual head honcho is Bryan Gray, MBE DL, who has been on the Board since it was formed in 2004 and is apparently good at adding up and taking away – which will hopefully ensure that the final bill to the Liverpool people doesn't have too many zeros on the end. The chief executive of the Culture Company, one Jason A. Harborow, who is also an executive director of culture, media and sport at the city council (so, who's his boss then? Warren Bradley, the council leader? Bryan Gray, the Culture Company chair? Colin Hilton, the council's chief executive? All of them? None of them?), continues to hang on in there, struggling along on a six-figure salary – his anonymity shattered by the Mathew Street fiasco and reputation confirmed when he was booed onto the stage at the city's 'birthday' celebrations. A minor revival in the Culture Company's reputation appears to have coincided with Harborow's departure on the type of extended sick leave that would see a mere flagger or street sweeper hauled off to a private medical and either laid off or assigned to 'lighter duties'. Such clauses, intended to 'protect' the employer, don't appear to apply to those on obscene salaries.

A perception pervades in Liverpool that public sector officers are not under the control of those whom the people of the city have elected, for better or worse, to direct them. Following on from 'Henshawgate' – when the city's paid chief executive, David Henshaw, infamously went to war with the council's elected leader, Mike Storey, leading to Henshaw's lucrative departure to well-paid employment elsewhere and Storey's departure from the leader's office – the apparent lack of democratic accountability exercised over the Liverpool Culture Company and, in particular, its chief executive has brought the city's democratic deficit once more into sharp focus. There is no little irony in the fact that Henshaw, then the nation's highest-paid local government official, on a salary dwarfing that of even the Prime Minister, was also occupying two posts; serving simultaneously as chief executive of both Liverpool City Council and the Liverpool Culture Company. Since each of the Culture Company's top bosses were also council officers, was there any need to create new job titles and give them another boss to answer, or avoid answering, to? Does having different job titles to cover different aspects of a post's duties somehow make the incumbent better at his job? Regardless of Phil Redmond's spin on the crisis at the Culture Company, likening public dissent and bickering at the top table to nothing more than a family tiff, there is widespread disenchantment, and a unique opportunity to engage Liverpool's lost generations (people blighted by an economic and social exclusion borne out of multi-generational unemployment and regeneration policies that sought to perpetuate the Thatcherite myth of trickle-down prosperity) may well have been lost.

In addition to using the o8 'brand' to package Liverpool's cultural and commercial 'product', Capital of Culture ought to have played a key role in the rejuvenation of the city's neighbourhoods – not that hard when you look at the relatively strong sense of community that still pervades in even the most deprived areas. This so-called 'social capital' could have provided the foundation for a programme that sought to instil a sense of belonging to something special in areas where the regeneration big bucks have yet to have any meaningful impact. Community projects in Granby and Everton limp along on meagre budgets, managing against all the odds to steer young people away from the lucrative and deadly trades that surround them daily. Local voluntary groups work valiantly against massive odds, and with absolutely zero recognition from the culture tsars, employing the attractions of music, art and sport to direct young people away from gun crime. Projects in rundown and under-staffed centres are drawing in people who the police would run away from unless they had a full Matrix team and helicopter to back them up. Yet in these times of wailing and gnashing of teeth over hoodies, guns and asbos, we continue to employ those who ignore the obvious and pour more millions into the pockets of the latest batch of urban renewal snake oil salesmen, all while we are jailing more of our own people than anywhere else in Europe.

Capital of Culture could, and should, have been a boon to such community-based initiatives. Almost every area of the city has produced someone of note in some aspect of the culture lauded in the 08 prospectus, be they sportspeople, musicians, writers, artists, poets, actors or whatever. Liverpudlians have been born into something special – let the younger generations and the 'excluded groups', whose abject conditions generate the big grant-funded executive salaries, know that this something special includes them and the city may yet thrive on the back of 08. Instead of the criminal splurge of other people's money on pie-in-the-sky feasibility studies – looking at the possibility of stunning all the fish in Salthouse Dock and moving them was an absolute belter – and multi-hundred thousand salaries, a meagre pump-priming investment would enable the likes of Positive Impact, a Liverpool 8 theatre company, to deliver profitable sell-out productions in Liverpool and beyond. Instead of cancelling the Mathew Street festival, the woefully under-utilized parks of north Liverpool could have hosted any number of outdoor stages. Local community music promoters, Rooftop Promotions, could have provided any number of bands to fill a local showcase stage. Mathew Street Festival in Everton Park? Well, the Liverpool Summer Pops went to another borough down the road!

Lille, the 2004 European Capital of Culture, took 15 buildings, one in each of the city's neighbourhoods, and developed them into cultural centres. Imagine such a programme in Liverpool. The city could have used the £5 million granted by the government for building work associated with Capital of Culture to attract European and other funding to fund the development of gallery space, performing arts venues, studios and rehearsal rooms in the likes of Kirkdale, Dingle, Garston and Croxteth. Raising horizons and building aspirations, releasing the next wave of cultural businesses and artistic output.

Such a programme wouldn't need to be grandiose, just sustainable. Upgrading the existing, neglected youth centre infrastructure would be a start, to provide, for example, modern recording and performance space – something delivered on a shoestring by Granby's Methodist Centre. Libraries and other public buildings, such as one-stop shops, could be adapted or extended to provide galleries for local artists and low-cost studio workspace. The 'expertise' at the disposal of the cultural elite could be deployed in supporting the work of local history and heritage projects, such as the Tourism in Vauxhall initiative. This fledgling industry could have been primed through the use of the Neighbourhood Renewal Fund grants that were misdirected into the 08 Place. Investment in the preservation of a number of key locally identified landmarks, such as Scotland Road's Old Bank, could help fill gaps in the provision of neighbourhood cultural centres in areas where no other premises are available.

To take the European Capital of Culture into the hearts of Liverpool's neighbourhoods would be a bold move, challenging an ingrained culture of exclusion and the resultant cynicism and suspicion of outsiders and officialdom that social exclusion inevitably breeds. In short it would require determination and it would require 'bottle'. A culture programme led by middle-class professionals and propped up by an impotent, largely aspiring petty bourgeois political class is hardly likely to collectively think 'Let's get down to Scottie and see what we can do there'. Would they have any idea of the Irish, Welsh, Italian and Jewish heritage of inner-city areas like Islington, Everton and Vauxhall? Still less, would they have the vision of someone like Ron Formby at the Scottie Press to see the potential for heritage tourism in such areas. 'The world in one city', so they said in the lead up to the award of Capital of Culture to Liverpool. The slogan, one that seemed to capture the hope and aspirations of a resurgent city, was ditched when the post-award logo was launched. Why? To dampen expectations? To stop the likes of Ron Formby from thinking his project had an economic future on the back of 08? Who knows, but the diverse communities of Liverpool 8 could be forgiven for thinking that the cultural richness that they could bring to a world in one city has been shunted out of the picture. Community activists in Granby have commented that when they receive visits from political and civic figures from local residents' various countries of origin, the visitors are shocked that the neighbourhood has no visible centre and no facilities for accommodating visiting delegations. As a result of generations of immigration and emigration, the Scouse Diaspora covers the world, nostalgia is big money, Liverpool's inner-city communities can do nostalgia and heritage all day and night. So, erm, let's build another tower block in town eh?

2008 could have launched the resurgence of Liverpool's districts. It would have taken vision and an unshakeable confidence in the people of those districts. Sadly, since the 1980s, such vision and confidence has been shunned in the corridors of power. Oh yes, there's been confidence a plenty shown in throwing ridiculous amounts of money around on expensive preparatory work for things that didn't happen. There's been a real confidence, that in the cases of Henshaw and Harborow has backfired spectacularly, in raising the pay and perks of public sector bosses to levels that have exceeded five, even ten times the city's average household income. The arrogance generated by such unwarranted wealth has led to senior public sector officers appearing to view accountability as a mere distraction. Rarely has this been so publicly apparent as in the sham of a public consultation that preceded the collapse of the so-called 'Fourth Grace'. In the first instance, a group of bigwigs on a lunchtime stroll decided that the Cunard, Liver and Port of Liverpool buildings were to be referred to as the 'Three Graces', then they decided they'd like a fourth 'Grace' to go alongside them. A competition was launched, the giants of the architecture and urban design world submitted proposals and a shortlist of four was drawn up to be put out to public consultation. The public duly consulted, Liverpool Vision (remember voting them in to decide what gets built in the city centre? Nope? Ah well) announced that the least popular option was to be selected. Apparently the consultation was only, well, consultative and the other three options were never feasible anyway! When the whole thing fell through and, inevitably, no single agency took the rap, it was reported that the non-existent Fourth Grace had cost over £2,500,000 of public money. Perhaps it's just as well we never got to have a say on what's currently going up on the Mann Island site – saved everyone the hassle of getting worked up.

In the ranks of senior and middle management, like has employed like, like has appointed like to the next panel, committee or quango down the line. The fallout of the hounding out of office, by the House of Lords rather than the electorate, of Liverpool's left-wing council in the 1980s has had a knock-on effect that pervades public life to this day. Such is the apparent fear of a resurgent left wing in the city among the aspiring 'professional' classes, such is the political class's mistrust of anything resembling fire in the belly, that passion and confidence in the ordinary people of Liverpool is seen as the last stage before a descent into revolutionary Trotskyism and is, therefore, to be avoided at all costs. The result: a timid and 'safe' avoidance of anything that might stoke up the flames of working-class aspiration in areas like Vauxhall, Liverpool 8, Anfield or Speke.

A near £70 million funding bonanza has been and gone in North Liverpool, with tens of millions more still flooding through in various guises, but in excess of 60 per cent of working-age people are still without jobs in Everton and the figure in neighbouring Kirkdale is stuck resolutely at more than 55 per cent. The brains behind this regeneration masterclass continue to ply their trades in ever more senior roles throughout the country. New Deal for Community, Housing Market Renewal, Urban Regeneration Companies, a plethora of initiatives providing rich pickings for the transient professional in an era of seemingly immovable social exclusion in many of Britain's working-class neighbourhoods. A poverty industry has been created where failure to tackle the conditions of deprivation that generate the grants and European funding in the first place guarantees plentiful career prospects as the funds continue to be ploughed in.

A similar story to that of North Liverpool can be told in the regeneration Valhalla of Speke Garston, where the worklessness rate hovers just below the 50 per cent mark. The people of Speke Garston will be proud that their regeneration was such a success that the genius who led them to such an abundance of riches, the one-time director of the Speke Garston Partnership, was selected to lead on regeneration across the whole city. Unfortunately, Liverpudlians no longer bask in the great man's reflected regeneration glory; he has moved to a top job with a firm that was awarded a major city council contract during his Regeneration Directorate. Common practice apparently, something similar happened with Liverpool Direct. As if things weren't bad enough for Speke Garston, their development company has been snaffled up by the rest of the city. The Speke Garston Development Company has expanded into the Liverpool Land Development Company and is now astounding Scousers with the vast number of jobs being created for the city's long-term unemployed in the so-called 'areas of opportunity' around Edge Lane, the North Docks area and Gillmoss.

What about the argument that 'these things take time'? That it's taken generations for things to get this bad so we can't turn the situation around overnight? Well, in the time it's taken Canary Wharf to go from derelict dockland shithole to global commercial epicentre, the Princes Park area targeted by Heseltine's post-riot crusade to save the inner cities has managed to achieve a jobless rate of more than six in ten. How the hell can this happen? How can hundreds of millions of pounds not make any real difference to the relative economic position of huge swathes of a city? Capital of Culture gives an indication of the processes that have been at work. The money is granted, local people get enthused and flock down to their community forums and agree a set of priorities, a board is elected and the priorities get prioritized. Then in come the big bucks and the people who will save the day for the poor of the parish arrive to 'manage' the programme. A delivery plan is drafted, in which the priorities become contextualized. It's now a year or two down the line and nothing appears to have happened; well we need to 'get the systems in place', don't we? Local people get fed up and only the hardy few continue to attend the community forums, mostly to spend time bickering with 'those who know best' about selecting projects to deliver the contextualized and prioritized priorities. A couple of 'gateway' schemes, some roadworks and a bit of CPO later, all the money's gone and so are the erstwhile regenerators, off to pastures new with a CV showing how they held those militant Scousers at bay to deliver spend targets on time. And so the cycle begins again, this time in Kensington – worklessness 51.5 per cent.

Every city needs outsiders, outsiders need the cities. But uniquely, Liverpool's ruling bodies appear to fear insiders. Community regeneration officers who don't go into communities have been a reality. The city's regeneration zones have witnessed the senseless and wasteful appointment of expensively relocated chief officers from all over the country who've subsequently been swiftly 're-organized' out of the way, only for another 'safe' pair of hands to be shunted into the breach. The cork being firmly pushed back into the local passion bottle until the next time it's needed to embellish a round of grant handouts. In this context the trajectory taken by Capital of Culture was almost inevitable, the script had been written and acted out time and time again over the previous two decades. Generations of like for like, safe and moderate, buildings and roads, had left a city used to false dawns, taking failures like the Fourth Grace in its stride, often laughing at the latest earnestly delivered proposal for a billion new jobs at the Stanley Dock and, sadly, shrugging its shoulders as another community follows the Boot Estate, Gillmoss, Anfield and Kensington into regeneration-led dereliction. In some quarters, principally those quarters where belief in the spirit and potential of Liverpool's people is weakest, this defeatist shoulder shrugging is seen as a symbol of apathy, as is the reluctance to vote in local elections.

Again, this demonstrates a complete misunderstanding of the culture of Liverpool, a culture described by Ron Noon, lecturer in History at Liverpool John Moores University, as one of 'diversity, dissent and a democratic spirit of involvement', otherwise referred to as the three Ds. When faced with an elected local authority that is apparently powerless to prevent its senior member of staff from briefing national government against council policy, as was alleged to have been a factor in the collapse of Merseytram; and an executive director of the council who can authorize the cancellation, at ridiculously short notice, of the biggest free music festival in Europe without even having the courtesy to discuss it with the elected leader of the council; and moreover, when control over hundreds of millions of pounds of local investment is entrusted to a cabal of appointees and placemen – then the shoulder shrugging and withdrawal from electoral politics represent, not apathy, far from it, but an active disengagement, a conscious decision not to legitimize the charade being played out in the city's name.

So why, prior to the cancellation of a boozy August weekend, was there no tangible rebellion from this city of diverse democratic dissenters? In the wake of the Toxteth riots a truly great Liverpool politician, the late Margaret Simey, herself the antithesis of timid and safe, rebuked weasel words, the comfort zone of diplomacy and sound-bite PR, to tell it how it was, stating unapologetically 'only apathetic fools' would not have rioted in the circumstances of 1981. Contrast this fearlessness with the Mersey Partnership's campaign to convince the nation's captains of industry that Ian Rush and Robbie Fowler were the 'only strikers' on Merseyside. A campaign launched just as 500 Liverpool dockers were catapulted into a bitter 28-month dispute, famously supported by the self-same Robbie Fowler! Posterity will determine who takes up the places in Scouse folklore; but don't bet against Simey and the ex-dockers (and, of course, Rush and Fowler) making the cut. Clearly Liverpudlians are not slow to articulate their opinions, yet generations of bureaucrats, consultants and assorted politicians, of most shades in a political spectrum from a pale washed-out scarlet to Lib Dem gold, have passed through the metaphorical hornets' nest and escaped with nothing worse than a couple of super-ficial scratches, compensated for by the superannuated salary and the CV entry that guarantees big bucks elsewhere. The answer to this dichotomy, where reputedly bolshie locals apparently stand by while the loot disappears from in front of them, lies in the tantalizing prospect of grant funding. All regeneration programmes arrive with the promise of funding for community activities. Capital of Culture is no different. Community organizations, traditionally the domain of the most active campaigners in Liverpool's neighbourhoods – particularly since the collapse of confidence in local government – therefore attempt to stay onside with the money men in the hope of securing much-needed income. For the most part unwittingly, some community organizations thus show a tendency to avoid critical observation of decisions they would ordinarily, without the teaser of possible funding, oppose with vigour.

In the case of Capital of Culture, organizations have privately voiced concerns or, as in the case of National Museums Liverpool, conspicuous silence has spoken loudest. However, for the city's arts and culture sector, 2008 is seen as just too big an opportunity to blow away in a big Scouse bust-up. Funding or no funding, this will be a once-in-a-lifetime opportunity to reach out to the biggest audience the city has assembled in its modern history. Coupled to this desire not to break ranks in front of the eyes of the world, organizations have walked the familiar 'staying onside' tightrope in the hope of eventually attracting funding for their o8 proposals. Nevertheless, cracks began to appear when local Labour Party leader, Joe Anderson, announced his resignation from the Board of the Liverpool Culture Company in June 2007, citing token efforts to involve the community, and 'wine and canapés' for VIPs among his criticisms of the company's efforts to date. Speaking to BBC Radio Merseyside, Anderson stated his concern 'that after a total spend of £94 million the legacy will not be a lasting cultural legacy or improvement in the cultural industry of our City. The legacy will be one of debt and quite frankly one of missed oppor-tunity.' In response to the Mathew Street fiasco, the Labour opposi-tion leader followed his resignation with a call for the abolition of the Liverpool Culture Company. The genie was well and truly out of the bottle, with even the eternally compliant Liverpool *Daily Post* turning up the heat for a day or two.

Staying onside is no longer an issue. In spite of the recent launch of two community grants programmes, there is now widespread accep-tance that the Capital of Culture programme will be largely city-centre based and will involve no significant neighbourhood activity. Certainly, the prospects of a North Liverpool heritage trail featuring highly on the itinerary of visiting American cruise passengers, or culture vultures heading into Liverpool 8 by the taxi load to see Positive Impact presenting the excellent 'Misunderstood' at a local venue, are remote in the extreme. In fact, it's not going to happen. There will be fireworks at the Albert Dock, probably more fireworks at St George's Hall and, because Liverpool always gets fireworks, the city can expect pyrotechnics to accompany Paul McCartney at Anfield and more than a few sparklers when the inadequate Liverpool Echo Arena opens its doors. The Empire theatre will polish up well for the occasion, as will the Phil. In fact, all the big stuff will no doubt go swimmingly. But what about the 'lasting cultural legacy' that Joe Anderson cast severe doubt upon? Is Liverpool 08 going to be the fur coat and no knickers Capital of Culture?

In fronting the culture lot up, Phil Redmond's clearly got it all to do! Can the decades spent in fear of stoking up working-class aspirations and expectations, of trickle-down regeneration managed at a safe distance from the 'problem', of timidity and like for likeness – can all this be replaced in less than three months by, not just a recognition of, but an embracing of Ron Noon's three Ds? In spite of Redmond's credentials and, judging from his excellent social commentary and ability to capture the mood of the day, firm understanding of the real, underlying culture of Liverpool, the odds must be firmly stacked against such a Herculean achievement. Clearly the allocation of expenditure to date cannot be undone, so any hopes of investment in local cultural infrastructure at the neighbourhood level will be in vain. Furthermore, the inevitable cost of the headline events will ensure that little is left in the way of revenue to provide the seed corn investment required to guarantee a viable legacy of cultural engagement. The official Capital of Culture programme, regrettably, will not give the city a Scottie Road Writers' Workshop to produce the next Jimmy McGovern, a Vauxy Theatre for the next generation of McGann brothers or the studio space for the seemingly never-ending conveyor belt of musical talent and innovation. Capital of Culture itself may not provide such facilities, but they might happen anyway...

Liverpool being Liverpool, and Scousers being Scousers, no doubt something will turn up! It won't be money, but then the grass roots have never had much of that anyway. If Phil Redmond's appointment is genuinely symbolic of a change in attitude, if not resource allocation, if there is a sea-change in the habitual 'professional' mistrust of proud Liverpudlian defiance and determination, then the culture mob may yet emerge with a modicum of credit in 2009. Through embracing diversity, dissent and a democratic spirit of involvement, politicians and officials will see a city spring into life. Instead of a cynical indifference, bordering upon a smouldering antipathy, Liverpool will put on its August bank holiday party face for twelve months and Scousers will gleefully take ownership of what was rightfully theirs anyway. Hopefully the examples of Edinburgh and Cork, where the cultural 'fringe' has eclipsed and effectively replaced the official mainstream, will provide inspiration for an arts and culture sector seeking to make its contribution regardless of the obstacles thrown down since June 2003.

Liverpool's regeneration is largely seen as having been kick-started by Heseltine's Inner City Task Force, launched in the context of a prevailing academic and political consensus that Liverpool was effectively finished. Geoffrey Howe, the Tory chancellor in 1981, was reported as favouring the 'managed decline' of the city, while leaked memos suggested that the government should play an instrumental role in the 'economic strangulation' of Liverpool, an 'attritional approach' intended to exhibit 'all outward signs of natural decline'. This war of attrition saw the city starved of resources. Tory Environment Minister Patrick Jenkin publicly exclaimed his shock at the state of housing in Everton while landmark projects such as the Albert Dock provided low-paid casual labourers with bit of work here and there. A walk around this tourist hotspot reveals where lads were paid to lay cobblestones by the hour (small gaps) and, later, by the metre (big gaps)! A lone, one-nation Tory amid a monetarist madhouse, Heseltine could see the writing on the wall through the flames of Liverpool 8 – give concessions to the blighted urban centres or the riots could turn into something far more serious; terrorism, even revolution. Regeneration, and the management of expectation, was born.

The starting point in Liverpool's true cultural renaissance will be a self-belief that acknowledges that we were right to stand up and fight the planned wind-down of the city. A genuinely resurgent and prosperous Liverpool will not be afraid of what makes it different: Diversity, Dissent and a Democratic spirit of involvement (thanks Ron!)

November 2007

Athens life ...
Family Matters

Karen Gill

❖

Karen Gill left Liverpool's stormy shores in the turbulent 1980s for a teaching post in Athens, Greece. Her grandfather, Bill Shankly, was one of the great flag-bearers for putting Liverpool bang-on-the-map. His stated case as a true Liverpool legend cannot be overestimated. His vision and passion were infectious and live on in the people who were around him and in those who 'really listened' and heard his words. I first met Karen before the European Cup Final in Athens in May 2007. I'm sure she is sprinkling some of her grandfather's 'bigger picture visions' to her Greek pupils as we speak.

I was dragged up in the 70s. Raised on 70s fare. Alphabetti spaghetti on toast, baked beans on toast and just for a bit of variation, ravioli on roast (never let it be said the chef lacked imagination). Anything that took more than three minutes to make was strictly off limits, and if it wasn't wrapped up in a tin overcoat, it was given a wide berth. You got home from school, buried your dinner in the back yard or threw it to some poor scabby stray (who more often than not, sniffed at it, then buggered off) and then you were issued with your instructions for the rest of the day: 'Get out from under me feet. Out you go to play.' You were summoned in around 6 o'clock, and then it was bath and bed (we started to revolt at the age of 13 when we were still being sent to bed at 7 o'clock!) You didn't dare disobey though, in case you got thwacked (a cross between a thump and a whack).

I've since forgiven my mum for these parental lapses; after all she was only 19 when she had me, and by the time she got divorced at the ripe old age of 21 she had another baby to look after. Where is all this leading I hear you say, what's it got to do with Liverpool and the Capital of Culture? Well, I didn't want to start with some sentimental waffle about how great my childhood was in Liverpool, how now that I've been away for eighteen years I look back with nostalgia on my formative years. The truth is when I left Liverpool at the end of the 1980s I couldn't wait to get away. Moving to another part of Britain was never an option. It wasn't just Liverpool that depressed me, it was the whole of Thatcher's Britain. The UK seemed to me a gloomy, grey place in the 1980s. Prospects seemed grim. The people I knew at the time were all on the dole, drifting through life, clutching their bottles of Newcastle Brown to their chest, drifting accidentally into parent-hood... always on the prowl for some scam or other.

An offer came up to teach in Greece completely by chance, out of the blue, and I grabbed it. I had only a vague notion of where Athens was but I had romantic visions of an ancient place with a long history, mythical gods on Mount Olympus and the hot Mediterranean sun. In the end it was none of the above that ensured I would not return to Liverpool the following year when my teaching contract was up. I taught Greek children at a language institute and to supplement my very meagre income I started to do private lessons. This meant I came into contract with lots of families and was able to observe them in the privacy of their own homes. I was gobsmacked! Talk about culture shock. At first I thought they were having me on. First and foremost, what assailed my senses (and perhaps naturally enough considering my vile culinary experiences) were the freshly cooked delights on the table every day. Now these might not necessarily have been cooked by mum; Gran was usually on hand to supervise in the kitchen, but it is also true that many mums do rustle up fresh meals every day. Sometimes they even bake their own bread and you certainly get tutted at if you don't make your own pastry for your homemade pies! Not a tin can in sight. Bliss...

The next thing to strike me was the closeness of the families. Children were consulted, advised and taken into account. Wherever you go in Greece you will see children with their families at tavernas, cafeterias (the English equivalent of the local pub), even the odd traditional Greek nightclub. I was amazed to discover that Greece is a child-friendly zone. No signs anywhere that children were not allowed. No Greek equivalent of the saying 'Children should be seen, not heard'. Often their offspring don't leave the roost till they marry. If they happen to get married in their thirties, it's still not peculiar to stay at home till then. I must admit I fell in love with this family-orientated culture. It was in such a stark contrast to my own experiences.

My grandad Bill Shankly died when I was 16 years old. He meant a lot to me. I adored him, he was the family anchor. He had always tried to press home the importance of the family. Unfortunately his career had not allowed him to play a very big role in his own children's lives, but he tried so hard to make up for this with his grandchildren. When he died it was like the family disintegrated completely.

Now in Greece I was confronted with his ideals of family life in practice. It instantly appealed to me. My grandad knew that a feeling of family isn't necessarily something you only experience with blood relations. He came from a close-knit community and he valued that sense of everybody working together and helping each other out. When he went to Liverpool he embraced the passion, the humour and the toughness of the Liverpudlians and he recognized that they were loyal people with an underlying sense of fairness. This was the combination that appealed to him: here were all the ingredients for a dynasty that has lasted till today and shows no signs of dissolution. You stick together, no matter what, but to do so you have to have guts (one of my grandad's favourite words, a quality he truly admired). You can't be selfish and just think about your own needs. You have to see the bigger picture, and sometimes it's hard. In my humble opinion and having had some experience of other cultures and people, the Liverpool people have definitely got guts. The Liverpool spirit is bold and intrepid. It's passionate and passion is inspiring.

I now came into contact with Greeks, some of them in their early twenties, who were totally obsessed with Liverpool Football Club. They had been inspired not only by the club and its history but by the passionate supporters they met on their frequent travels to away games. I think that this is the point at which I felt the wheel had come full circle. My grandad had sown the seeds, I had seen the beauty of these ideas in practice and now I had come into contact with my new 'family' in a country thousands of miles from my own. Some of these Greek fans, rather amusingly, even had the hint of a Scouse accent when they spoke English and their vernacular was peppered with Liverpool slang (one time I nearly sprayed my retsina everywhere when one of the lads said, in relation to getting tickets for the Champions' League match... and I quote: 'There's nottun down for ya girl'). It's always comforting for me to hear the Liverpool lilt and my ears always prick up when I catch a whiff of it. My children have a slight trace of an accent, which is always more pronounced after a few weeks at home in West Derby! (Their mother tongue or Ma tongue is Greek so it sounds really sweet when they speak English anyway.) The last time my 10-year-old son came over to Liverpool with me, we went to a Liverpool v Man Utd match at Anfield. For months after I couldn't get him to stop chanting 'You fat bastard' in a thick Scouse accent!

The razor-sharp Liverpool humour is legendary and is perhaps one of the things I miss most about home. I always look forward to a visit as I know my cheek (and bladder) muscles are going to be well exercised. Greeks have more of a Benny Hill type humour which just cannot compare with the quick-wittedness and pithy repartee of the Scousers. Greece is a very orthodox country in more than just the religious sense of the word and such conformity can be very comforting, but I have to confess that more and more I miss the 'fluidity' of my hometown. Liverpool, like the river, is always in motion, is never static; it's a city on the move. It rejects conformity and has a healthy disregard for authority. There's a fierce sense of localism but at the same time our eye is on the horizon. We can see the bigger picture.

Nothing will ever fill this Liverpool-shaped place inside me; nothing will sever the umbilical cord that attaches me to my birthplace. People who were extremely important to me lived and died there, and when I think of my mum and grandad, that's where I picture them. Now they've gone, but I feel that the family has expanded rather than decreased. I know that there are things to dislike about Liverpool but the bottom line is; family matters… a lot and you stand by your family no matter what. You see the negative aspects but you feel fiercely loyal and protective of it; after all, it's about seeing the bigger picture and I feel my grandad and Liverpool blessed me with that vision.

2008

Halewood life …
The Sound of the Suburbs

John Garner

❦

John Garner is a man I have known for donkey's years as the last man to bulge the net in the Spion Kop goal. John, a plumber by trade, writes in his spare time. Married with two daughters, he attends numerous local gigs while enjoying the odd pint of lager. John states a favourite pastime as being in the company of good Socialist people and organizing the coach he takes to most Liverpool FC away games. Leather Bottle Ultras is a flag you may have seen inside and outside a large number of European stadia. Like JG, it travels…

Who could forget that famous day when Liverpool's well-heeled and elected/unelected gathered round the big screen in the Empire theatre, eagerly awaiting the announcement of Capital of Culture 2008? The sheer pandemonium and emotion as the winning result was sensationally given, breaking Geordie hearts and Birmingham's rather optimistic spirits. Council leader, Mike Storey, and people's 'champion', Sir Bob Scott, hugging each other as if their favourite team had just scored the last-minute winner in the FA Cup Final; two grown-up representatives of this fine city wildly celebrating the cultural rebirth of the UK's most put-down citizens…

'This is it!' many must have thought. 'Just wait for the jobs to come out of this one.'

'We'll have the gig of the century never mind just for 2008!

'Where better?'

'We gave you the Beatles, let's get something back…'

Well no actually. Most people you speak to in the suburbs of Halewood, a forgotten part of the region south of the city, speak of the general distrust of all things Capital of Culture. An area devoid of a basic shopping area for its local people, an area where its local boxing talent has no permanent home. 'Get the kids off the streets', well fine, give them somewhere to go. An area where the local authorities have overseen the closure of four local community public houses, including the renowned Leather Bottle... real cause for celebration that then?

Come 2008 it would be nice to jump a bus into town to take in some of the advertised events, but don't bother trying to get a 78 bus after six o'clock, cos there is none. You could always use the hourly train service though, if it turns up of course! Maybe the people of Halewood would sound a tad bitter to an outsider; there are worse places to live in the Merseyside area after all. But there are also not many places that have had to put up with utter betrayal by their elected bodies.

Is the European Capital of Culture victory just for the big-wigs and the elite of Liverpool, or do the minnows and underdogs of the surrounding areas really stand a chance? And are the elected council-lors doing their jobs by ensuring we are actually given something to celebrate? A sense of involvement would be nice...

A celebration of the Arts perhaps... Forget it. The area not only lacks basic amenities but exists with no outlet for theatre or associ-ated activities. Fancy putting on that production that the local drama group painstakingly brought together? Put it on where? Ah yes, but the Liverpool Philharmonic Orchestra play every other year in the local sports centre? Well, no actually, they don't any more since the local sports centre was down-sized and the new one hasn't the capacity... shame that.

Maybe the powers that be are holding back on something. The local schoolkids are not going to be excluded. We are going to be pleasantly surprised and McCartney's gig at Anfield in 2008 is going to include a free night for thousands of youngsters, irrespective of the ability to afford an extortionate entrance fee of £55 (with an 11% handling charge of course!) Cheers Macca! Proper Scouser that...

You know what? Maybe we should have seen all this coming; after all, who ever trusts a Liberal Democrat, especially in this place? Was it hard for you to truly believe that the city's salvation had finally arrived after years of neglect and after decades of gross mismanagement by the ruling bodies? I know as I took the victory jigs in, my distrust for all things Capital of Culture was always bubbling below the surface. A false dawn? Probably. A wasted opportunity? Definitely.

Thank God then for the one thing that truly unites the working class in this city, the saving grace and the epitome of the ordinary citizen here... football. Surely Liverpool and the soon-to-be residents of Knowsley, Everton, have something special planned, a celebration of all things Merseyside, a show of gratitude for over a hundred years of dogged loyalty? Don't hold your breath. Would it really be asking too much for both clubs to get together and organize a celebration exhibition match, a special thank you to 'the people' who made them what they are now, multi-million pound sports giants in a European arena, while 'the people' are still living on handouts from the EU, in areas still classed as officially poor?

We are regularly fed the spiel that the whole concept of Capital of Culture is that it's the people who will make or break it, Liverpool people are unique, loyal, friendly and thoroughly deserve the accolades being thrown at us... well, give us something to look forward to then, let us control our own destiny. The people of Halewood deserve better, from their council, from the local evening newspaper, from local industry. There's a party going on down the road this year and they're being made to feel like the proverbial gatecrasher.

Oh for the halcyon days of the Jubilee in '77, when even the anti-royalists among us could tip their hats to the efforts that went in to organizing that. Meanwhile this lot couldn't organize the proverbial piss-up in the local Cain's brewery... sad. Of course, I know I am sounding a bit too parochial, it must be the same for many areas on the outskirts of the city, Kirkby, Huyton, and so on, but I can only talk from our own experiences... and they leave a bitter taste in the mouth for those Scouse residents from L26 – all 25,000 of them.

Let's hope the next batch of local talent gets due recognition and gets that mother of all invites to the party. A little help from the pot wouldn't go amiss... I presume all money available will be splashed out equally? Maybe if I was a playwright from the Wirral or North Wales I could apply on behalf of the good and great of Halewood for a handout? After all, the whole shebang appears to be hijacked by a mishmash of pencil pushers from the South and other areas that have as much connection to Liverpool as we have to Manchester's next failed high-profile sports extravaganza!

So when the call goes out and we are expected to drop everything and celebrate the biggest party in this place since the ending of the Blitz, spare a thought for the mere residents of one of its many council estates... we'd love to come, but we've got fuck all to wear!

2008

Cultural life ...
Cock-ups and Pasta Sauces

Neville Skelly

※

Neville Skelly is a singer I have known for the last couple of years. A passionate believer in Scousers and his native city, I once saw Neville take the compere's job last minute at a local charity do for the Hillsborough Justice Campaign. He not only carried it off with aplomb, along with others, I now have him earmarked as a compere of future events.

Paul McCartney is coming to Liverpool to play Anfield Stadium. Fucking big wow! (Oh, and by the way, hopefully the people of Liverpool will get the chance to see him and the tickets won't get snapped up by council employees like last time.) Meanwhile, Ringo Starr's just stood on top of St George's Hall in his astronaut coat and given a two-finger peace salute to the world's media at the launch! In the words of Ricky Tomlinson's alter ego, MY ARSE! The people of Liverpool should give a two-finger salute of a different kind to those responsible for the holy fuck-up that has been the Culture Company regime since the day we were awarded the prestigious opportunity of being Capital of Culture.

My hope is that when the Culture Company is wound up and the executive salary train moves on, we don't look back on this as a missed opportunity to leave a long-standing cultural legacy for the city; a way to showcase its indigenous talent and show the world what we are truly made of while not relying on ageing rock star relics from yesteryear – stars no longer relevant to today's generation. Yeah, it has a place, but the emphasis should be on new talent; unearthing a new generation of writers, artists, musicians and so forth. By not getting young people from deprived areas involved, or finding out what Liverpool culture means to them by engaging them, I feel we have missed a big chance. There should be a buzz about 2008. Scousers should be proud and excited, having had input and feeling included. This is sadly not the case.

I can't help thinking if John Lennon was still alive he'd have wanted to have been in there from an early stage, getting involved and putting something back, not just jogging in for the limelight and fuckin' off again on the next private jet out. How much is Macca getting paid for the showpiece Anfield concert? I bet he won't be doing it from the goodness of his heart!

Like most Scousers I was appalled by the killing of Anthony Walker. Coming from Huyton, I have seen first-hand how environment and ignorance can on occasion manifest bigotry and racism. So I had an idea for an anti-racist concert for this year that didn't go ahead largely due to apathy and lack of interest from the Culture Company, who said they couldn't offer any financial support. It would have been an amazing concert full of current Liverpool bands like the Coral, the Zutons and stalwarts like Ian Brodie. The reason they gave was that they already had a big concert at a newly proposed purpose-built stage at the Albert Dock. Guess what??? It had to be scrapped because it was not financially viable. So there we have it. It took four years and thousands of pounds in feasibility studies to finally find out that it wasn't viable!

That is the level of incompetence I'm on about. Any Scouser on the streets could have told them it was a ridiculous idea. And that is the point! Instead of the Culture Company people being sat in plush offices, they should have been out engaging Scousers, getting on the streets, or talking to people alongside or through a media campaign, instead of all the cloak and dagger bullshit and keeping everything hush hush. This is not sour grapes by the way because the anti-racist concert may still go ahead at Anfield, as the staging and infrastructure will be there. I'm hoping we'll be able to tie it in around the same time.

The list of cock-ups to date is unbelievable. Robyn Archer, appointed as Creative Director because she had delivered international events, had to be removed (or left for personal reasons). It should have always been a Scouser, or at least a team with the expertise to give a sensational and brilliant showcase of Liverpool talent.

The fiasco that led to the Mathew Street Big Stages being cancelled did real damage to the city's reputation in the lead up to 08; another example of mismanagement of the highest order. We eventually found out it was down to cost-cutting and budget reduction. The Mathew Street festival – one of the most successful free music festivals in Europe! Embarrassing, yet life goes on.

People can only do a job to the best of their abilities, within the confinements of their role, but the more tiers of bureaucracy involved, the harder it is to get anything done. When you have a scenario where people are in the dark and no one knows what is happening, chaos, mismanagement and overspending ensue.

The Culture Board should be representative of the people of Liverpool. They did a great job in the bid to be City of Culture 08, but that was just the start, not the end. When the shit hits the fan regarding cock-ups, who is accountable? Nobody takes responsibility in politics. A scapegoat is usually found in the form of a person who is expendable or has least to lose, or who has left already, so making them an easy target.

A new Culture Board should have been elected by the people of Liverpool. Candidates could have included some of the city's talent in media, music, film production and art. Those who have a capacity for getting things done, innovators with vision like McKeown, McGovern, Russell, Kenwright, Bleasdale, Barton… I could go on. Look, I don't know Loyd Grossman personally, but what the fuck has he got to do with Liverpool Culture? He's fuckin' famous for making pasta sauces!

The appointment of Phil Redmond may be one positive to come out of the Mathew Street fiasco. I had numerous meetings with different people at the Culture Company, including Gordon Ross, who told me that they had decided they weren't going to commission an official song for 08. One of the first things Phil got the public involved in. Seeing as Liverpool is also comedy capital, why not put Ken Dodd at the top of St George's Hall and commission a statue of him while he is still alive: a fitting tribute to a real Scouser, one who still lives here and loves Liverpool. Starting out in the music hall era of entertainment, Doddy's a one-man cultural legacy to treasure. Point being: Capital of Culture, City of Mirth – let's just hope the joke's not on us.

Love life …
Sweet, Sweet, Emerald-eyed Punk

J.M., written by Nicky Allt

⊰⊱

J.M.'s a long-ago mate I re-found in a Liverpool boozer one weekend. We used to argue over the football, but now older and wiser… we still argue over the football. When we were running wild around Europe and started dressing differently J.M. used to go to some Liverpool games with me, and vice-versa. No bitterness in those Scouse camaraderie days. He pissed off to Aussie and the world for years and I was surprised and buzzin' to find him back in his Liverpool home once again. He's a councillor now, and after asking me to write this for him (I really enjoyed the story), I told him as a councillor who couldn't write he should do well (it was a wind-up). I hope he finds some power in the council as he was always an honest Scouser. Some used to say… too honest.

> *For the record*
> *J.M.'s favourite Liverpool things:*
> *Band: Echo and the Bunnymen*
> *Liverpool book: Her Benny*

An Everton game in winter, followed by a bowl of his Ma's Scouse with red cabbage and burnt crusty cobs from Sayers. There you go – J.M.'s food choice – something I finally agree on with an Evertonian. Gerrin there!

Stood in a two-inch puddle of urine my new suede desert boots were soaking up some Welsh punk rocker's cloudy piss. I'm thinking, *deffo been on the snakebites.* Resting both hands on the wall above he drunkenly released the night's intake. He was blubbering to himself in Welsh. The patch-painted wall, autographed in felt tip by every unsigned band in the North of England, had dropped mouldy paint peelings into the urinal by the dozen. Pulling out a black marker he carried on pissing while adding his own moniker to the collage. Something ending in dragons… I couldn't make out what he'd put. Don't know why he bothered, it'd be peeling off within the next 24 hours. Like the toilet wall, the floors, in fact the whole club, he looked a mess. Eric's was a complete dive, but it was the only complete dive in town to watch the bands we loved. When I say complete, I mean that in the ramshackle state it was in it somehow seemed complete.

99 per cent of Liverpool boozers wouldn't play this music, or anything that riffed, jumped and kicked with boots on. It was all soft-shoe-shuffle-funk, and groovy white-boy soul and disco shite. With Detroit shuffles and Harlem city nights abounding, for a musical city by the sea the narrowmindedness of Liverpool DJs and their night-club bosses was bordering on cultural fascism. It was why we put up with standing in piss nearly every week. Those posher gaffs, Tuxedo Junction, Scamps and the Hollywood were *Saturday Night Fever*, three-button-open, tarted-up sausage factories. A place for Girobank Debbie from Old Swan to finally meet Prince Kevin from Huyton, after she'd had her tights around her ankles from Hillside to Halewood with every last frog in town.

Another punk, six-foot odd, a safety pin rammed through his scabby bottom lip, half-smirked at me. He began singing the Clash's last song in a cocky, loud-mouthed manner. Here to watch the same band, far from bevvied, I eyed him steel toe-cap to grotty string vest. I couldn't go any further with his roughly pricked lip bulging with green pus. He returned the look as if to say, 'Who you fuckin lookin at in our club straight boy?' They made me laugh these sneering, half-arsed Billy Idol types; waiting, posing for a passing photographer who never, ever arrived; forever trying to look New York City tough after Mummy had washed and ironed their bondage Kecks for them.

Our little mob had started dressing differently than everybody else, with straight-leg jeans, button-down shirts and polo tops added to sports windcheaters or Harrington jackets. We were getting called smoothies, straights and football boys at first. It then changed to scallies, and eventually we got labelled as casuals by the slow-as-fuck Southern-biased media. When we'd visit other towns and cities for concerts, or for Everton and Liverpool games, the locals gawped at us like we'd just beamed down from planet 'What-the-Fuck'. From late '77 through the whole of '78 the main Eric's members would look us up and down like it was their scene, their music – like we'd side-swerved the guest list and bunked into *their* own little private world of Anarchy by the Mersey. Now don't get me wrong, some of those punks were alright, but most were bigger poseurs than any baggy-looned loverboys or the footy kids I knew.

Around the time nobody dressed or acted like our little crew (200 or so young Everton and Liverpool fans), but punk meanwhile had become an identity for Richard from Widnes and Judy from the Wirral to wholly re-invent themselves. The Sid Vicious sneering pout that the phony Billy Idol got by on for years should have been renamed the Surbiton glare, or, in the best punk club in the North: the Formby gawp. Behind that stare usually lay a student from the suburbs trying to act like a tough guy rock star. Or underneath that heavy black mascara, females who were acting 'the Nancy' from the Sid and Nancy relationship had been practising disco numbers with expensive hair dryers as microphones a year earlier in their mum's Stag bedroom suite-mirrors. I had a good natter with one feller who thought he was Marlon Brando in *The Wild Ones* reincarnated. The daft twat was from Heswall and didn't have a clue if the actor was dead or alive.

As I say, a lot of serious reinventions going on in tatty ol' Liverpool in those days... funny though. I bet those same Liverpool punks who commuted then preened their anarchy pose to perfection later became councillors and city officials. I mean, how else could you explain such a large number of arseholes in one collective body – a body that seemed hell-bent on smashing whatever was good in Liverpool to smithereens. Communities, ace buildings, the original Cavern... it's endless. Sometimes, myself, I think it was the revenge of the punks!

If a lot of north-west punks were middle-class commuters from the Wirral and beyond, the footy kids were working-class, born and bred Scousers. Some were Park End blue, some were Road End red. It didn't matter to us. Leaving the piss-stenched bogs behind, the Clash song 'Garageland' could be heard bouncing off the ceiling. Joe Strummer, intense and giving it the bifters – as usual – screwed his face to spit the words. Mick Jones jumped about adding vocal and guitar, his gaunt persona cutting a true memory-framed, rock star figure. Backing the two front men a spiky-headed Paul Simonon held and played bass with that low-slung, gunslinger technique of his, while Topper Headon on drums looked like a worn-out, punk rock smackhead with the extreme workouts he was getting being in this band – a band we all loved. Eric's walls were dripping wet like always. This was a club that needed gutters inside. The intro to 'White Riot' entered the dinghy shithole and the place went mental.

Pushing through to the middle I almost lost a piss-stained desert boot in the process. Looking to the front, middle-stage area a fight had broken out. Thinking nothing of it, as Eric's punk brawls were more frequent than Liverpool City Council cock-ups, I carried on pogo'ing like Zebedee from the Magic Roundabout, been sprinkling speed on his shredded wheat. Once the song finished and raucous applause bounced off the rafters, a lone blonde kid lay on the floor with blood around his forehead and face. As it began to seep into his hair and drip from the tip of his nose, the music stopped. The three white stripes of his Adidas training shoes glistened under the glow of the stage spotlights. Scanning closer to where he lay, I realized it was Anthony, a good Liverpudlian mate of mine. Shouting to the others, I steamed over. A large, heavy chain with a padlock at one end lay nearby his head. It looked bad.

A young punk girl wearing a Clash City Rocker tee-shirt pushed through to take her faded denim jacket off, before pushing it under his head. Looking at her I never spoke. She had the most gorgeous green eyes. Magnified close-up, like sparkling emeralds trying to dodge behind the heavy black make-up she wore, they drew me in. An undoubted hidden beauty in this club, her natural dot-to-dot freckles made her seem like a New Wave Celtic goddess, beautiful and unworldly. Speechless, for moments, even with Anthony unconscious, I stared into those mint-greens mesmerized. The moment she let go of her jacket a huge punk rocker slammed to the deck nearby.

Bernie C, a lad who often drank in our crew, had started decking anyone who looked threatening – most punk rockers could look threatening if they felt the urge. Bernie's fighting motto was that if trouble broke out he'd go straight for the biggest feller on offer. Part bravado, part youthful invincibility, true to his word he got locked up inside Innsbruck's Olympic village a few years later, after decking a muscle-bound Alpine ski-monster who attacked him with one of his skis when he tried sliding down the Olympic slope in a pair of Adidas Samba. The punk rocker had fallen to the ground like a huge oak tree chopped at base. Seconds later, pandemonium broke out all over the dance floor – if you could call it that. The footy lads gathered quickly. Their numbers were fifteen, tops. I stood over Anthony, guarding him from people joining the affray. Next thing, the smirking Welsh punk from the toilets had lamped me on the side of the head. Quick-tempered, I was in. The lovely green-eyed punkette tried dragging me back by the Levi belt loop. She tugged so hard it completely tore off. From that point testosterone and gang mentality took over. Though it seemed like ages at the time, the fight probably lasted no more than two minutes.

Bouncers separating the two warring factions instantly blamed the footy lads, ejecting them onto the pavement. Spilling out onto Mathew Street, for a short time it looked like a battle between a group of San-Fran college preppies and a be-chained, leather-clad, LA biker gang. With the biker gang carrying chains on pants and coats, not in hands, they backed off into the sweat and steam of Eric's, the bouncers slam-locking the door behind them. With Anthony still inside some lads started attacking the door.

After a minute or so it flew open and he tumbled out into Mathew Street looking groggy. We sat him down on a derelict wall opposite. He mumbled that he'd had an argument with a pogo'ing punk rocker who'd told him he hated local lads like 'our type' coming in to a New Wave club. When Anthony had asked him what our type meant, he replied that he'd been beaten up by lads dressed in trainees, jeans and Fred Perry sports tops last weekend. Apparently we looked like them. The argument got heated about punk ideals, dress codes and whatnot, till he basically pulled out a huge chain and struck Anthony across the temple. Anthony said the feller had told him he was from North Wales like Mr Piss-on-yer-shoes. Surmising there must have been a load of North Welshmen over for the Clash gig, we patched Anthony up by washing the two-inch gash and huge lump with one of his socks dipped in a cold pint of lager. Peter T would fight the world while keeping one eye on his beer. He wouldn't leave his ale behind in any circumstances. Putting his Adidas training shoe back on, Anthony said he felt okay except for a bit of a headache. With no time for sympathy or pain, we gave him some stick about falling asleep on Eric's dancefloor and the night carried on.

Later that evening we ended up at the Swinging Apple, a sort of punk-come-dump nightclub that stayed open till dick docks. Along with Michelle Claire's the only other one in Liverpool at the time – I think. Entering the main area in a semi-drunken haze, Talking Heads' 'Psycho Killer', dark décor and some slow-dancing punks let you know immediately that you were in no Kevin-and-Debbie disco dive. Some of the punks openly had sex in the bogs and on the stairs. It was like stepping into the land of the weird and wonderful – if you liked that type of thing, that is.

The animosity between punks and smoothies was always on show, and often bang in your face. It was a young, young people's dirty-stop-out gaff, where the décor and interior meant sweet fuck-all and the music and staying out meant absolutely everything. Often I'd stop and just take it all in. It was like 'Clowns to the left of me, jokers to the right, here I am, stuck in the middle with glue'. Yeah, the carpets were either full of last week's lager or last week's sponk stains! Take your pick. Usually with an expensive pair of trainees, your new pride and joy, you'd be watching out for puddles or mud, but in this gaff you were looking for clear white tile and trying to dodge any dark, murky carpet.

Once drinks were ordered and the sham that was Sham 69 hit the turntables with 'Angels with Dirty Faces', I locked eyes with her again. Green-eyed Punkette was dancing that reggae-ish type slow-dance that the punks would do to numbers like Ian Dury's 'Sweet Gene Vincent' and the Clash's 'White Man in Hammersmith Palais'. Thinking she'd fuck me right off I sauntered over for a closer look at those eyes and freckles. I've always given a third and fourth look to a naturally freckled beauty. On about the fifteenth gander by now, she still looked stunning. Fit-as-fuck but not knowing it made the loveliest girls lovelier still.

Approaching, she smiled mid-dance. The punk lad nearby stopped. I thought, *here we go*, till he revved his Doctor Martens into dancing mode again. Reaching into her long, lacy glove she pulled out something. It was hard to see among the smoke and poor light. I moved closer as she waved me in. In her hand lay my missing Levi belt loop. She'd torn it off completely during the affray. Looking for the green light in those emerald eyes, she smiled. I moved closer still. God... she was fucking gorgeous! I mumbled something about why she kept it. She answered that it was in the eyes. Lost for words and not wanting to quiz or spoil anything I took her hand without thinking about it. We walked to the stairs hand in hand, and, funnily, I didn't give a shit who was watching. On her feet she wore cheap, black plimsolls; above, black leggings underneath a short black mini-skirt. On top, a white Clash tee-shirt with a battered bleached Levi jacket whose top pockets held numerous badges: 999, the Damned, the Stranglers, etc.

Around and on the staircase, couples in clinches writhed openly, some only a zip away from the make-a-baby stakes. Two lip-sticky girls kissed nearby, their tongues on open show performing a lesbian loop. Asking emerald her real name, she asked me did it matter. I told her no. She asked my name. I asked did it matter. We laughed and locked lips simultaneously. Her velvety mouth tasted of liquorice. Once we stopped kissing, and believe me I could've happily necked away all night, I asked about her taste. From a denim pocket she pulled out a bag of liquorice all-sorts. We laughed again. I asked could I take her home, she said she would love me to but it would be impossible tonight. At 4:15 am I reckoned it was morning, not night. She started to panic, saying it was time she made her way to the coach she'd travelled in on, and would I walk her there. Confused, but not wanting to push things after the night's aggro, and with her transport set to leave from nearby Chinatown, we upped sticks.

Leaving the Apple, stepping over bodies, the Stranglers' 'No More Heroes' faded away behind the club door. Hitting the street, Chinatown stood a couple of blocks away from Liverpool's main clubland. I'd had girlfriends before but I'd never walked along the street holding hands with one. It normally felt poncey to me, but here I was more reluctant than her to let go. Newspapers blew wildly down the jiggers while empty beer bottles and cans clattered in the glazed morning-night. The wind whipping up from the Mersey made me want to snuggle into her. Me wearing only a Fred Perry tee-shirt, Levi jeans and Adidas training shoes, we looked an odd couple. People were very dress orientated and partisan to their own group. I was more aware of this than most. Some drunken stag-night suits walked by, commenting on her appearance. I told them to 'Fuck right off'. She laughed at my tempestuous way. Unmoved by their comments, she had spirit alright. Here I was walking along Wood Street at four in the morning with a punk girl whose name I didn't know, but whose mere presence gave me goose pimples whenever I thought of getting close to her.

Noticing a half-full coach ahead but not wanting our time to end I pulled her into a back-alley and started kissing her forcefully on the lips. In the city centre, we were so, so alone. Loving her liquorice taste, the Mersey whip lifted the hairs on the back of my neck as I tried to fumble with her buttons. Grabbing my hand she told me no. 'No?' She was a punk girl. I was surprised. Weren't they all supposed to drop their drawers at the flick of a safety pin? Telling me it wasn't the right time or place, she said her coach would be leaving without her. I told her to let it go. Asking did I have my own flat, I told her not to be ridiculous. She shut me up by replying that if I never had my own place, then asking her to let the coach go was me being ridiculous. She was right, of course. On our final steps to the coach doorway I asked could I see her again, she answered she'd love me to. Nervously shivering, more than aware of my rapidly spreading goose pimples again, I enquired about her phone number. Putting a finger to my lips she said a small carry-out bag on board held a pen inside.

Boarding the first coach step, the driver looked at me disdainfully. Going through my James Dean phase I returned the sullen look. Some punks tried to get past me but I didn't want to take my eyes off her. They aggressively pushed past, all elbows, zips and leather. Catching the back one's eye, I sussed it was Piss-stain. He ambled onto the coach and sat next to his boisterous mates. I knew immediately it was the Welsh mob we'd been fighting with in Eric's. Mumbling between themselves, suddenly seven or eight lads jumped up and stormed to the door. Standing my ground, I knew they could only move single file. Hanging around too long, a huge pair of ox-blood Doctor Martens missed my cheek, glancing off the top of my shoulder. Stepping from the coach, taxis headed away down Berry Street and George Street. Looking for local support, the bleak city roads were deserted island grey.

Stood shouting down at me, it was as though none of the punk mob wanted to make a move. Two more approached from behind. The ones aboard finally stepped down. I was off. Speeding through South End of the city jiggers I could hear clumpy boots hitting cobblestone. Thing is, once I was gone to the up and running stage, with no fingers clasping cloth, I was long gone. You've heard of Linford Christie, well I was Christie Linford without the two pound of sugar.

Back at the Swinging Apple the club doormen were lashing people out onto the street. That's exactly how it seemed as the heavens opened. Chasing inside past a couple of lashing bouncers, I told them I'd lost my taxi money inside. Traipsing upstairs, my footy amigos were long gone. Not wanting to be trapped inside a stinking nightclub I bounded back down the steps two at a time. The punks were already swaggering back up the cobbled street. The bouncers shouted out, asking if it was me they were after. I replied yes. Telling me they'd told them and their Welsh accents to fuck off back to waltzer-spinning duty, I thanked them profusely and began to walk behind the silhouetted group – keeping distance of course. Soon as we reached Slater Street I sprinted left and up into Bold Street, which ran parallel with Wood Street where the punks walked, and all the way to Chinatown and, hopefully, the lovely freckled face of Emerald-eyes. Top of Bold Street, near the bombed-out church, I had to sprint the hundred yards or so down Berry Street to bring the vast cathedral on my left and Chinatown on my right into view.

The coach idled kerb-side, its exhaust coughing clouds at the Chinese restaurants. The sweet aroma emanating from one basement eatery was rudely interrupted by chara-fumes. I loved both smells but they didn't mix. Empty coach seats told me I'd beaten my pursuers back to their transport. Walking around the charabanc I caught sight of Emerald-eyes. Creeping up to her window I was glad to see she hadn't closed those twinkling beauties and fallen asleep. Tapping at the glass I got her attention. She smiled warmly, trying to blank out her fellow passengers. Soaked through, the Mersey whip blew a gust straight up the back of my Fred Perry tee-shirt, making me shiver and shake like an Elvis puppet at Christmas.

Due to the bus being an old St Trinian's rust bucket, I'd noticed an outside handle on the emergency door at the back. Tracing 'phone number' on the window and with my lips, she produced the magic note, waving it at me with that sweetheart smile of hers. I'd been thinking skylight air-vent stories, but it was an awkward an' a half move that one. Again, using miming lips while pointing, I spelled out back seat. Once she understood and moved to the back of the coach I was ragging at the chrome handle. Praying it would open, we only needed the briefest contact. At first I tried gently pulling it down. It didn't budge. Yanking it hard with two hands it dislodged. The emergency door flew open. I couldn't see inside the carriage but faces at the windows above let me know they were onto me. A delayed alarm went off, alerting the miserable sad-sack-of-a-driver to what was going on. In the early morning hours it sounded like the foghorn from the night boat to Cairo. She threw me the piece of paper. Senses unbalanced by brew, I missed my catch as it hit the floor. Turning around, four or five Welsh whoppers had left the coach to confront me. Sweeping up the piece of paper I ran at them. They backed off momentarily. I carried on running towards them, dodging directly around their group at the last minute. I was off again.

Sprinting up Upper Duke Street below the vast shadow cast by the cathedral, out of reach, I sauntered up the hill backwards, clocking the departing coach coughing fumes in the distance. That split moment of mob indecision had given me the green light and Green-eyes' phone number. Underneath the magnificent cathedral, fenced off from its grounds, a prostitute approached offering me business. On the prowl, she looked sunken-cheeked, ghostly-white and half-dead. Her black eyes preyed upon me like a vampiress out on blood-sucking duty from a tomb in the nearby Dracula castle. No thank you, Miss Wank-you. Taxi please!

Getting back to Walton where I lived in the shadow of the prison walls, I put my older brother's *Abbey Road* album on the turntable and pulled the tattered piece of paper from my Levi pocket. Being soaked through the ink had run. Putting it under a warm sofa cushion to dry, I drifted off with George Harrison reminding me of Emerald-eyes by singing 'Something in the way she moves…', only to be woken by my Ma asking angrily what did I think I was doing putting records on at half-five in the morning? An argument broke out – as usual – and my Da appeared to calm things down. Usually the other way around in most households, in ours my Ma was the kick-off Mike Tyson and my Da, the peace-making Mahatma Gandhi.

I'd been battling with my Ma on and off for about two years now, but this time Mike Tyson was right. I'd been staying out all hours, bringing girls home, leaving my room like a shit tip, and generally acting like a lad who needed his own space to fart about and mature in. My Da had boxed to a decent standard when he was younger, and had disciplined me and my three brothers continually since we were infants. Outside the ring he was peace personified. Most people referred to him as Gentleman Jim. He'd gotten three sons from four to box, the odd one out being me. Rebellious in spirit, with a confrontational persona and temper akin to my Ma, it seemed all me and her ever did was go to war. Being headstrong had already gotten me into trouble with the law three or four times, and, to be honest, a few hours in the cells and a slap on the wrists meant I was soon repeating the same mistakes that got me collared and cuffed in the first place. My Da said me and her were serial energy wasters.

That week I went into a flat agency in Bold Street where I'd chased up to Chinatown the Saturday before. Within a week I was the tenant of an empty-except-for-a-bed top-floor flat in Sheil Road, Kensington. Phoning Green-eyes, she told me her name was Janie and that she lived in Colwyn Bay on the north coast of Wales. Though I was a trainee surveyor who could hardly afford to miss Saturday overtime – especially with my new furniture shopping list – I took the day off and jumped a National bus out to see her when she told me she had the house to herself that weekend. I never missed a match at Goodison, or away from home, but for her, and because we were only playing boring Norwich City, I took the gamble that we'd get on as well as we did in our semi-drunken haze that rainy night in town.

Meeting me at the bus station her red hair, freckled face and eyes all looked aglow. Her soft Welsh accent sounded sweet compared to my coarse Scouse. Often when we see, become aware of or touch something good which, for whatever reason, becomes out of reach, we can tend to overstate its goodness, beauty or importance. Romanticizing something is one way of putting it. Then, when we finally get it into sight and grasp hold of it, we can become slightly disillusioned or even wholly let down. My little Saturday dream was no let-down. All the beauty I thought I'd seen was right here in front of me.

Once we reached her house on the hill, with her parents away on another hill in Snowdonia, we laughed, loved and danced the whole weekend long. Most of the household furniture was covered in sheets, with sealed carboard boxes heaped about the floors. When I enquired why, she told me they were upping sticks to Liverpool soon. Her dad was a doctor and he'd been offered a post at the Royal Liverpool Hospital. More music to my ears, I wondered why she hadn't told me that first night. Anyway, this was all the incentive I needed to dance around the house stark-bollock-naked. And I did. For two days all our favourite New Wave bands played non-stop on her small record player. A weekend love-in that you didn't want to end. I asked her why she'd stayed with me and given me a chance after I'd been fighting with those other Welsh punks. All she'd say was that she could see beyond all that, and the real me was right there in my own eyes. Janie, eighteen – oh so wise for one so young – was an instant gold-framed imprint. I went home on Sunday evening, back to an empty flat, knowing I'd found someone special. I didn't see her again for ten whole years.

❧ ❧ ❧

An End to Violence

The following weekend after my love-in with Janie, and after we'd spoken at length on the phone every night, I went to watch Everton play Coventry away. After a narrow defeat I left the ground and got split from my mates. Walking through the park at the back of Highfield Road, I saw a large football disturbance taking place between Everton and Coventry supporters. As a lot of young away fans did in the late 70s and early 80s I ran over to get involved. When I say a lot, I mean mass mobs of youths. You either did or you didn't, but around those early punk end of glam-rock days most football lads did. Always game, I ran straight to the heart of the brawl. As the Coventry crew started to run away we chased on after them. Catching my mate Stevie, more

game than most, he told me to keep up as this sky-blue punk rocker
had lamped him one and he badly wanted revenge. Now the feller, in
baseball boots and skintight black pants, could run, but so could we.
Chasing onto a housing estate we followed closely behind. Wearing
a yellow Sex Pistols *Never Mind the Bollocks* tee-shirt, he'd cornered
himself by darting into a street with a huge wall that created a dead end.
Hurtling down the block-paved driveway of a small semi-detached we
menacingly followed him in.

Passing a rusty old banger parked on the driveway, we stepped into
the back garden. Skinny as a pipe-cleaner and taller than both of us,
he tried to climb over next door's fence. Densely covered in climbing
plants, you couldn't tell if it was a wooden or brick divide. Unable to
get a grip he turned to face us. Picking up a child's plastic Noddy car
he threw it at us – missing by a mile. As we moved into attack, grasping
that he had nowhere to run or hide, he bellowed a final 'fuck off' before
dramatically diving to the floor. Stevie and I looked at each other
bemused. We'd expected half a battle. OK, an unfair two-onto-one half
battle, but still a battle. Lying motionless, with the two of us stood over
him, he suddenly kicked out a long leg in a sweeping arc, wrapping it
around my legs to bring me down. Thinking it was some kind of Kung
Fu move and that we were dealing with a Karate Punk, I laid into him
on the deck. His spidery legs were wrapped around me as I started to
lash out. Stevie started hitting him from above. He stank like a tin of
baked beans been left open in a dog kennel for two weeks.

Rolling about with Johnnie Snake Legs I was getting dirty and
smelly till Stevie landed a shocking hook to his ribs. He wheezed like
a fifty-a-day pensioner and let go. About to carry on the attack, voices
behind shouted to stop. Turning, an upright officer of the law and some
people from inside the house stood watch. You could tell they were the
owners as the back door was open, while others peered through the
kitchen window. The copper was already on his radio. Panicking, we
tried to climb the fence that the long-legged punk had just attempted.
Meanwhile, he was writhing on the ground holding his ribs, crying out
for somebody to help him. It was a big act, and this punk rocker was
drama-smart as he laid it on like a South American footballer looking
for a last-minute penalty. Rolling about the grass, bumping into my
legs, I kicked them forcefully away. The bizzie shouted, 'Hey, it's over,
that's enough!'

Elbowing Stevie, I muttered 'Just go for it, he can only grab one
of us'. The bizzie spread his arms as we moved forward. Sprinting

towards him we only had the narrow gap between the garage and the garden to slice through. Conscious of the fact that it was looking like we had to scale the fence or we were nicked, I made a grab for a large wooden pole holding up the washing line. The bizzie stared on. 'Now don't be silly lad, you'll only be in more trouble.' Backing off slightly, the daft twat thought I was getting ready to lamp him with the pole. I could be stupid at times but not plain thick. Running at the fence, I dug the pole into the turf and vaulted towards the flowery barrier. Flying though the air I noticed red brick through a gap in the fauna. It was too late to change my direction, or mind, as I sailed a foot over the top. I'd got it just right – an Olympic special. As I threw the pole across to Stevie, the bizzie, knowing he only had one lad to deal with, moved in for an arrest. The gangly punk rocker was still doing his best Marlon Brando by writhing about on the floor. What a tithead!

By now most of the neighbours were enjoying the show. An old lady, staring at me from her bedroom window, smiled as though we were the evening's entertainment. I nervously smiled back. Running along the patio and around her house I unlocked the back door. Chasing to where we'd first entered, I now stood behind the lone bizzie and the home owners. With the street being a Berlin-walled dead end I only had one way out. I didn't want to start fighting with the bizzie, or leave Stevie. Thinking on my feet, my mind was made up when a rapid response unit showed face. Slamming the brakes, four uniformed officers jumped from a side door. Badly wanting off, there was nowhere left to go, except straight at the cops or back in the garden I'd just come from. The garden was a trap. Running straight at the uniforms I dodged the first one, till two black boots came flying across my body to scissor me to the deck. I couldn't believe it! The copper in question had performed a flying kick on the concrete to send me to ground. What a hero! Probably Coventry's Chief of Police by now.

Spreadeagled, face-down, munching tarmac, I was roughly hand-cuffed and put into the pig wagon. A minute later Stevie was brought in. When I asked Sergeant Drop-Kick where gangly legs was, he told me they'd called an ambulance after he'd said we jumped him because he was a punk. It seemed to me he was suffering with a bad case of memory loss, not punky broken ribs. Though I'd have laid good money on the fact that he was blagging, we found out a couple of weeks later from hospital reports that his ribs were really bust when we were charged with GBH and violent disorder. Kept in custody till the Monday after the Coventry game my head was so upside down that

I never phoned Janie till the following weekend. The phone line came back dead. Thinking jittery fingers had phoned the wrong number, I tried again and again. The phone had been disconnected. I'd lost her. It did my head in almost as much as the looming court case.

Our hastily acquired solicitor was a pinstriped buffoon on a jolly down to Coventry for the day. With Mr Oxbridge Useless thinking about his stamp collection, not our case, they decided to make an example of me and Stevie due to escalating hooliganism at Coventry City's Highfield Road stadium. We were given six months each. It felt a little over the top, but when reports came in about me and Stevie's previous and our solicitor defended like Titus Bramble in stilettos, we were a done deal. My Ma and Da were gutted, my extended family and friends upset, and my employers cold and unsympathetic – sacking me for breach of apprenticeship and gross misconduct. Me, I was heart-broken, angry and dejected all in one sentence.

After a few Big-house mishaps I left the gates of a shithouse Midland nick roughly twelve weeks later. Unemployed and fed-up, I'd also lost my flat and over-riding weekend joy for the football. Going the game never felt as good after that. Why? I suppose, basically, because I had to behave myself and act the Mr Go-lightly. Football and following Everton was about stomping around the football grounds of the country and pushing the laughter boat out as far as you could. When it came to simply watching poncy footballers performing better roll-overs than that gangly-legged punk, I couldn't be arsed. Going to the odd game, the lads, noticing how uninspired I'd become, started referring to me as the Lifer. They reckoned after three months' jail I'd changed beyond belief, like I'd just got out after a seventeen-year stretch.

Meanwhile Stevie was back at the games full-tilt, stating with bravado that he'd been longer on a message. Over the coming years he went on a few more six-month messages, before finally receiving an eight-year one for wounding with intent. I think some people get indoctrinated into the dark jail system and some people see the light through the cell bar windows. Always an illuminated light merchant and hater of anything claustrophobic, I'd chosen the surveying trade for one reason only: it meant outdoors. Now my job was gone and trade unfinished I needed to find a future that kept giving me light. My Da had called me a serial time-waster; well… twelve weeks of having to waste time endlessly had given me more than a short sharp shock, it had shown me a side to life that was dark and unforgiving if you kept on driving down a certain road.

Concerning finding Janie, I got as far as jumping the bus to Colwyn Bay in search of those emerald eyes. Finding her beautiful house on the hill, the new owners said they'd been left no forwarding address by the previous occupants but they knew the family had moved to Liverpool. Strange eh? You meet a girl, she lives miles away. You visit, you enjoy. She moves to your hometown, you can't find her.

Welcomed home by my Ma, I knew the hoo-ha wouldn't last. Soon as the arguments started up, with me bringing home girlfriends on dole money, I knew I had to do the Jack Kerouac and hit the road. A mate, Ian Mac, was off to Jersey to get work on the building sites surrounding St Helier. Within a week the sun was shining me all the light I needed, with the two of us ensconced in a two-bedroom, curtain-less flat above a shop. Jersey is a beautiful island, but for me it seemed small and claustrophobic after a while. That summer of 1980 I had one long party while moonlighting as a painter and decorator, receiving cash-in-hand and signing on at St Helier unemployment office to pay the rent. Those lovely beaches in places like St Brelade's, St Catherine's and St Ouen's Bay... full of Nordic language students hot to trot. Jail, heartache and football seemed a distant memory as I worked and spent and met female holidaymakers on a nightly basis. For a short time it was marvellous. In the winter I joined other Liverpool migrant workers by heading to Sydney, Australia. Like a lot of Scousers I had family in Oz and they helped me settle into decent accommodation, instead of living in shitty digs with the rest of the migratory mob down on touristy Bondi Beach.

For the next four to five years I lived the Jersey-summer, Sydney-winter lifestyle and had myself a bit of a painter's party. With border control lax and not as riddled with terrorist paranoia as it is today, I skipped the light fandango with a paint brush in my hand, decent money in my pocket and a host of beautiful girlfriends to help me forget about sweet emerald eyes. Hankering for a bit of hometown Scouse humour I interspersed my have-brush-will-travel existence with a visit home every six months. With Scousers working in every port I'd visit, the call of home was diluted by the many Liverpool people I'd meet on my travels. I came home to see Everton win the League Championship and Cup Winners' Cup in Rotterdam, and for Cup Finals against Liverpool and Man Utd. Noticing that my old mates were always skint, it kept me striving when the call of home grew loud. Working in Jersey, Australia, California, Colorado, then Jersey and Australia again, I eventually landed a trainee draughtsman's job in

Auckland, New Zealand. Here I lived till 1989 when finally the call of home became a bellowing shout I heard most nights in bed.

Checking the local *Echo* that my Ma and Da sent me every couple of weeks I applied for a draughtsman's job back in Liverpool. By phone and letter I amazingly got a top job back in my place of birth. I was buzzing. New Zealand was a lovely country, full of open space, lakes, countryside, you name it... but it wasn't Liverpool. I came home after working away for nigh on ten years, the week before Everton were about to play Norwich in the FA Cup semi-final and one of my brothers was about to be married. It seemed like perfect timing. My gypsy steel toe-caps were thirty years of age and I was wise enough to know that I couldn't gallivant forever. House prices were on the increase (what's new?) and I wanted on the ladder. Moving back into my Ma and Da's was OK for a couple of weeks, but the prison that loomed near home forever reminded me of being trapped and that you should never step back. That house was my safe ship in the harbour, but that wasn't what ships were built for. I needed to voyage in and around Liverpool. That was the new option. I wanted success where my heart lay. Full of optimism, this time things were going to be different.

At first things didn't go as planned. The job didn't pay well and the fixer-upper I'd bought in Broadgreen seemed to be taking forever to become move-innable. With me slumming in the shade of Walton Prison, Everton won their semi-final at Villa Park, putting them into the FA Cup final at Wembley. Seemingly I'd returned home at exactly the right time, till any glory became totally overshadowed by what had happened at the other semi-final between Liverpool and Nottingham Forest at Sheffield Wednesday's Hillsborough stadium. Ninety-six Liverpool supporters ended up losing their lives that dark, dark day, on what for Evertonians was supposed to be a day of triumph.

A huge crush at the Liverpool end of the stadium was caused by an inadequate Police Chief (Duckinfield) deciding to open a main gate into the ground to relieve crowding outside, resulting in a surge into an already full ground and people being trapped. Once people were trapped inside a tunnel that led onto the viewing pens (yes, fenced-in pens) and they tried to escape the horrendously claustrophobic situation by moving forward onto the terracing (those same overcrowded pens), with no police or stewards on hand to usher them to the half-full side terracing, those already inside the middle section were jammed into the front wall with the freedom of the pitch cut off by huge wire fencing. Eventually a barrier collapsed and along with the many injured and traumatized, ninety-six of those furthest to the front were crushed to death. Nobody ever admitted culpability, though the Police Chief had ordered the main gates to be opened. The flames of injustice still burn bright in Liverpool today.

A young cousin of mine – injured enough to be hospitalized – brought home the reality of football being just a game. Released from a Sheffield hospital, he had to visit the Royal in Liverpool for some further tests. Visiting one day, with the city still in mourning, he'd been told he could go home that evening as everything looked fine. Being one of the only people in our family with a car, I'd been put on stand-by to pick him up whenever it was time to leave. A nurse began helping him pack away his belongings as I waited outside the ward. As he smiled at me, he gave a knowing wink over her shoulder as if to say, 'Have you seen this nurse, she's gorgeous'. Unable to see her face and being nosey, I made my way over.

Not realizing that I'd been waiting outside she heard me enter and turned, telling me it wasn't visiting time yet and could I wait outside. Offering an apology, followed by an explanation, I gave a longer look than normal as my cheeky cousin nodded approval. Staring straight back, her look lingering too long for comfort, I tried holding her gaze till she eventually blushed alongside a faint smile. A light sparked inside me the moment she turned away. Her red hair, strikingly tied up inside her white nurse's bonnet, her gorgeous freckles and those piercing green eyes; so alive as they mirrored the beams of mid-afternoon sun that filled the room. It was Janie and those sweet, sweet emerald eyes. She was as she'd been photographed into my memory: beautiful. A hush fell over the room as I knew she'd recognized something in me, but how much and what I didn't know. I spoke. 'I know you don't I. Janie... isn't it?'

Turning, she smiled. 'Well it took you a long time to get in touch.'

'I got arrested. You moved house.'

'How do you mean you got arrested?'

'That week, when I told you I was going to Coventry to see Everton.'

'But you had my number.'

'Yeah, but they kept me in custody. Then you'd moved.'

'Ah, so you *were* a little scallywag after all.'

'Yeah, but you stuck by me that night after the Clash concert.'

'Yeah, I know, I told you it was in the eyes.'

I couldn't believe she remembered everything after all the years in between. My younger cousin stared on speechless, unable to fathom the knowing conversation. We sat at the edge of the bed to talk some more, while he wisely for one so young took a walk to the toilet in the ward corridor. She'd been married five years ago; divorced two years later. She had a daughter aged two and quizzed me about whether or not I had kids of my own. I told her about my worldly gallivanting, with no time for a serious relationship. She said she envied me. I told her I envied her. She asked why. I told her nobody in the world where I'd travelled had eyes like hers. She blushed, offering me that gorgeous smile. In an instant I was back inside Eric's and the Swinging Apple all over again. I told her I had to take my young cousin back home to his waiting parents, but I'd love to meet up and talk with her sometime. She told me she was a full-time staff nurse and could I meet her for lunch the following day. In like a shot, I wanted to hug and kiss her there and then.

I met Janie the next day. She'd been living in West Derby village the whole time I'd worked away. Her accent had changed. The accent in North Wales is slightly similar to Scouse. Now she sounded Scouse. Walking down London Road, away from the Royal, we stopped at the magnificent St George's Hall before sitting on a bench in St John's gardens behind the building. As the seagulls swooped and hollered I asked her if she'd ever given me a thought. She replied she had, on several occasions. It felt good to hear her say those words. Aimlessly walking past the Mersey tunnel entrance she told me it reminded her of that night, as the rusty old charabanc had headed back to North Wales through that gaping hole in the floor. Walking some more we carried on up Whitechapel before cutting through into Mathew Street. We knew where Eric's doorway had been and where those punk posters used to advertise the next band in town. Looking into those sweet, sweet emerald eyes of hers, I put my arms around her and kissed her full on the lips. Just one hour of her company and one day after finding her again after ten years, it felt like the most natural thing in the world. The goose pimples were on show, my heart skipped a beat, yeah, yeah, all that crap. But you know, they may be clichés and they may sound gooey on paper, but when all is said and done, and when all those macho layers are stripped away, it's all we've got isn't it: some love and good feeling. Anyway, it felt good to feel those feelings at thirty years of age. Lucky to find my soul mate, and luckier still that she was beautiful and unattached, I never lost sight of her again and we were married seven months later.

The reason I've told you my Liverpool love story is that today, sixteen years married, I'm on my way to becoming a Liverpool city councillor, and if I had a pound for every established councillor who told me he used to go to Eric's and used to love the same bands as me, then maybe I'd be able to buy a nice flat in this new town of ours and still have some change over. It's funny how a dingy old nightclub within a shabby old building can gain some sort of mythical status that everybody wants to make out they were a part of. With new glass buildings going up all around and the Liverbird resembling the Phoenix as this new city rises from the old, I think about how I almost missed out on seeing those mint-greens again and how life can be strange, and maybe, just maybe... some things are meant to be. If regeneration and culture are part of the new zeitgeist then I was lucky to be able to regenerate a bond that is now an integral part of my culture and, truly, something I couldn't imagine living without.

Three kids on, with my step-daughter fully grown, Janie and I laugh about my version of blaming the ex-punks for a lot of Liverpool's wrongdoings. Nobody knows about my jailbird past and my couple of years as a nailed-on football hooligan and, hopefully, they never will. But listen, hey, if they do, they do. No big deal. Part of growing up, part of who I am, my short time in jail put me right back on track. A short, sharp shock! Something sadly missing today, as I tearfully read of little Evertonian, Rhys Jones, being gunned down at eleven years of age as he played in the street. That little kid had his whole life ahead of him and now it's been sadly taken away, as once again, for me, liberalism takes its toll.

People like me needed to be answerable, and with parental and authoritative control being undermined year by year, a complete turnaround in the teaching of respect for other people is what we need to finally put an end to anarchy on our streets. Yes, I was a young scallywag, but I knew, or was taught the difference between right and wrong and black and white. Now, that shaded grey area in between has become a way to abuse the system, and right and wrong have become shaded words themselves. For me, they should always remain clear and precise. I know, because like I said, their preciseness put me back on track. No clearly defined lines and heaps of liberalism and you end up with a mess and moral decline. Liberal attitudes to certain things are fine, but concerning moral behaviour, punishment and respect for other human beings they should be carved in stone never to be tampered with.

Living in the same area where the shooting took place and, as my beloved football team cast a vote on a move to Kirkby, and change is rife and shootings are often a weekly occurrence, I wonder if I can do some good in the city where my heart lies. I'll never leave Liverpool again. Once you've lived here it never really leaves you. I had to travel the world to get to know my hometown. Now I'm back on my streets, I feel I do. Returning home, I was lucky to have found Janie and, in so doing, I found myself. If this is my culture and this is the new Liverpool in culture year – a city where a young life can be taken so easily; a place where people need to re-educate their youngsters, tomorrow's adults; and a place that may seem strange without my beloved Everton FC within its boundary walls – then I owe it to my city and my people to embrace change and to try and make a difference.

July/August 2007

Cultural life ...
Bureaucracy vs. Creativity

Peter Hooton

-᠅-

Peter Hooton is a feller I have known for years. Lead singer of the Farm and one of the main pioneers of the fantastic End *magazine, he has never been scared to put his head above the parapet to try and do things for the good of his city by looking to create and be creative. The Farm's biggest hit was 'All Together Now'. If only our councillors could heed those three words and stick unswervingly to their meaning we would be ship-shape as a city within five years.*

It's very easy to be cynical isn't it? As Liverpudlians we have it down to a fine art, we are conditioned to be suspicious of outside accolades, of condescending awards and patronizing plaudits. We have heard it and seen it all before but nothing had prepared us for the Capital of Culture pantomime! When we were first awarded the title back in 2003 most people seemed to shrug their shoulders and mutter 'so what', as people had been conditioned by Garden Festivalitis two decades earlier.

Television footage showing bureaucrats and politicians celebrating 'Olympic winner' style persuaded some that it would be churlish to be dismissive. Anyway we thought, doesn't Liverpool like to party, whether it is at christenings, communions or funerals, so at least it will be one big knees up! However, four years later, after untold monies squandered on fat salaries for people from outside Liverpool dictating what our 'culture' is, I think Liverpudlians are definitely asking 'What the hell is going on?' In a way I'm proud that we have been noncommittal from the start. The judges declared that Liverpool triumphed over Newcastle, Birmingham, Bristol, Oxford and Cardiff because of its people. The first thing the faceless unelected bureaucrats (who nobody can name) did was marginalize the people!

Now we all know that not everyone can organize an event and

wait for that pot of gold to be granted, but the general consensus and word on the street is that the people are not only being ignored but are being dismissed as well. Whether it's bad management, incompetence or just plain stupidity I cannot pass judgement, but let's face it, our City Fathers have a good track record when it comes to the aforementioned – they knocked down the Cavern, demolished the Overhead Railway and would have blown up the Albert Dock if it hadn't been built so well. What about the proposed tram system, the Fourth Grace and the recent Mathew Street debacle?

Bring back Cases Street and the Liverpool Stadium and demolish these sterile glass buildings and loft apartments, or at least flatten them and turn them into car parks!

Bureaucracy – the death knell of creativity!

2007

Cultural life …
Capital of (Popular) Culture

Dave Kirby

━❦━

Dave Kirby went to the same madhouse school as me and we have known each other since were about sixteen. We both wanted to write, and often spoke of this whenever we bumped into each other over the years. With me gallivanting all over the world I didn't bump into the same people that often, but whenever I was back in Liverpool Dave was a face I'd always have a gab with, and that gab reverberated around literary talk and if we were ever going to do something. I hope we already have…

When the announcement was made that Liverpool had won Capital of Culture for 2008 I must admit I punched the air – not exactly in the same way I'd celebrate a Liverpool FC goal, but elated just the same. The hopes I had when I punched the air that day have turned to wild punches of frustration and disillusion.

It's all about that word 'respect'. If people from outside the city come here to work or study and embrace the culture then they'll be welcomed with open arms. If they come with their own agenda and show contempt for what's here then they'll be run out of town. We are a cultural melting pot – a city made up of English, Celtic, Nordic, Welsh, Italian, African, Asian and other cultures – all of whom have weaved the fabric of what we are today. We are different. We have more in common with Dublin and Glasgow than we do with other parts of England. Our Celtic roots are firmly embedded in humour and music but for some unbelievable and worrying reason the word 'entertainment' is frowned upon by some in the Liverpool arts world.

I wholeheartedly respect and support the need for diversity for 2008 but sadly that respect and support isn't reciprocated by certain members of the Culture Company and other artistic institutions. Whether they like it or not populist culture is what put this city on the worldwide map. Thousands of visitors will descend upon us in 2008 enjoying our wonderful treasures such as the Walker Art Gallery – World Museum – St George's Hall – two cathedrals – Albert Dock complex – our unique Georgian architecture – the fantastic Philharmonic Hall and orchestra. But you can bet your sweet life that the queues will be twice as long for a slice of Beatles and football culture.

Local involvement with an understanding of populist culture at the script submission stage of Liverpool theatre is absolutely imperative. Liverpool has an insatiable appetite for entertainment. As somebody who worked at the wheels of industry for twenty-seven years I know all about the need for and importance of entertainment as a form of escapism. To the vast majority of Liverpool people, all escape routes are populist – whether it is sport, music, comedy or film. But unfortunately there are those who'd prefer 2008 to be twelve months of intellectually challenged profundity. Any form of elitism is abhorrent – high art elitism is no different. I truly hope that one of the legacies from 2008 will be an attitude change towards populist culture.

2007

Writer's life ...
The Capital of Kidneys

Sarah Deane

❧❦

Sarah Deane, born in Liverpool in 1972, is a writer I have known for a year or so. Striking me as the kind of person who has the capacity to go on to great things in a literary sense, she has worked in the gaming industry designing fruit and quiz machines for fifteen years and is now a freelance quiz compiler and scriptwriter. If she's got the staying power to take her big chance when it finally comes along, I'm sure she will. Sarah has written for TV and is in the process of getting her first novel published. Living on the periphery of the city centre and being single she is in the jammy sodding position of being able to write whenever she bleeding well likes! Get on with it then Mrs, we all know you're gonna be famous one day.

I am a religious girl, have been all my life. I used to go to my church in Anfield every Saturday at 3 pm sharp for the 90-minute service, but in recent years that's changed to 12.30 pm or 5.15 pm, Sundays at 2 pm or 4 pm, even midweek at 8 pm. But it's not about what's convenient for me, it's about the greater good. I'm happy to pay my £40 fortnightly fee to worship in this place (I sometimes pay another £40 in the weeks in between at our 'sister' churches across the country), because I like to sleep at night knowing the church is being maintained properly and the clergy employed there have enough to eat (I have regular nightmares about them starving in the gutter as I know that £50,000 a week per person doesn't really stretch very far). Often I get to thinking that not all of the people who work there are as committed to the cause as I am, and sometimes I even find myself wondering if it's all been just a big confidence trick and me and my money have fallen victim to a great big bunch of charlatans (I know I'm too trusting), but we all go through periods of doubt and reflection, it's human nature and just part of the 'test' sent by the big man (who's Scottish) to weed out the weak from the strong.

Anyway, I've got pots of money to burn, so it really doesn't bother me if my subs go up once the new church is built in a few years time on Stanley Park. In fact, the more I can give, the happier I'll be. After all, what else am I going to do with all this cash? My mortgage is so cheap I've got shedloads left over once it's paid every month. My supermarket bills are a doddle, too; I don't know why people moan so much about the price of this and the price of that. Do they think that the very ordinary, just-like-us Sharon Osborne can afford to do those Asda ads for free? Of course she can't. The money's got to come from somewhere, and I for one am delighted to contribute.

I'm also lucky enough to own a Ferrari that runs on fresh air, and Liverpool City Council only charges me and the other 96 people in my building £120 a month each to empty our collective four bins about once a fortnight, and we don't even have to bother with all that recycling shit either, it's one bin for everything, it's great! And when I go to the shops, I enjoy jumping over the paving slabs that protrude upwards about six inches from the ground at three-feet intervals, trying to trip me up. It's free exercise, which I'm extremely grateful for. It's similar to the game of 'chicken' I play every day when I try to cross the road at the 'new' pedestrian crossing on six-lane Islington outside Staples, a 'magic' crossing that must be invisible to drivers as it's only the people trying to use it who seem to know it's really there.

Apparently, this crossing won the Most Dangerous Place In The World (That Isn't Iraq) To Put A Pedestrian Crossing 2007. Impressive or what? As I've always said, a trophy is a trophy is a trophy. How I laughed the other day when a woman nearly got her legs sliced off by a Ford Mondeo as it came racing round the corner from Moss Street, ignoring the red light in front of him. Silly woman, I was thinking, you really should have been faster there, crutches or no crutches. That car was only doing fifty, hardly Lewis Hamilton is it? And just because the green man says it's safe to cross the road, it doesn't actually *mean* it's safe to cross the road, he's playing with you. I've often had a laugh about this with the numerous beat bobbies I encounter on my daily strolls, comforted in knowing that my money is being invested by the People in Charge in the safety and wellbeing of its citizens. I just wish they'd take more money off me. It's all going to waste otherwise.

Which is why, after helping to fund the NHS for twenty years through a very reasonable rate of tax and national insurance contributions that I can more than afford (tax me more, please), I wasn't particularly concerned when, recently, I was unfortunate enough to go down with an infection. However, because I don't *get* ill (hangovers don't count), I ignored it for three days, before thinking it might be an idea to seek some help. Lying on my bed screaming in agony had been the first clue, but when my standard cure-all of two Nurofen and an orange juice didn't work, I knew it was time to take action. No worries, I thought, there is a state-of-the-art surgery around the corner, I'll give them a tinkle and see if I can have a short chat with, oh I don't know, a doctor perhaps.

I won't bore you with the whole story, suffice to say I now know that it is the receptionists, not the doctors, who decide whether or not you need medical treatment, based on a simple, but conclusive, telephone personality test. If they don't like your voice, even if you're crying down the phone in pain while you speak, you've no chance of getting a slot (a plea to anyone who lives with a doctor's receptionist – DON'T piss them off before they leave for work. People will die.)

That night, as I hallucinated, I was trying to distract myself from the pain by throwing wads of banknotes from my window and watching the urchins of Everton fight each other for them in the street, and also by playing internet Scrabble (*stabbing* 26 pts, double word score; *agonise* 8 pts; *forgodssakekillmenow* 0 pts 'Sarah, that's *not* a word and the board isn't big enough anyway....'), when an email pinged its way into my inbox. It was from my friend, Chris. 'Here's the table of events for Capital of Culture, loads of stuff to get involved in!' Sure enough, I opened the document to find a detailed itinerary from the *Liverpool 08* committee, outlining numerous 'cultural' events to really put this city on the map (Bleasdale, Russell, Merseybeat et al. having made a rubbish job of it the past forty years, evidently).

I won't mind admitting, I was rather excited about seeing what the People in Charge had in store for us, especially Sir David Henshaw, who I'd felt sorry for ever since those nasty Lib Dems scuppered his intention to pocket a £350k pension and a tax dodge the size of Knowsley back in 2005. Some people are just jealous. So, with Big Dave on board, I could be reassured that 2008 was going to be all about Liverpool and nothing whatever to do with Dave securing a Baronetcy. What an incredible opportunity this would be for Liverpool to well and truly 'show off', big style. So imagine my disappointment when, fifteen minutes and two more Nurofen later, I was still trying to find something in the events list about Liverpool *by* Liverpool.

Well at least we were hosting the 2007 Turner Prize! That annual shit-fest (in fact, you could submit an actual pile of shit, and be knighted for it five years later) where mad people 'create' stuff and even madder people debate its place in society against the price of fish. The key to judging something like the Turner Prize is simple. The crapper and more artistically worthless the exhibit, the better it is. If you can explain what's in front of you without using the words 'conceptual', 'zeitgeist' or 'antidisestablishmentarianism', then it's obviously rubbish and won't win. Still, I'll keep an open mind, which in itself could be a winning entry for 2008's competition. There's also a *public art installation* programme planned to run throughout the year, which includes a project called *'visible viruses'* which, I assume, would involve parading a small child with measles through the streets of Wavertree or something.

Also, and this is before 2008 even kicked off, there was *'the ultimate Nativity'* for Christmas 2007, *'the story of the first Christmas as told through the music of Liverpool'*, which was fantastic, as I thought Christmas had been banned ages ago for being offensive to non-drinkers. Or was it non-Christians? I can't remember. It was on the telly and everything, quite spectacular. But as long as they didn't go all fundamentalist and mention 'Jesus', I assume it passed off relatively peacefully.

My whole body was still killing me as my eyes then landed on something called *'Waiting'*, described as *'a creative health and wellbeing programme which brings arts and creativity into health care centres and hospital spaces... it explores what happens to us when we wait and how this experience can be different by changing our internal space and our external environment... this programme is jointly funded by the Liverpool Culture Company and Liverpool Primary Care Trust.'* If anyone can understand a *word* of that, well done, have a cigar. But, limited though my understanding of SpeakingBollocks is, it seemed to me that, instead of employing more doctors, opening more surgeries – in short, giving us what it is we're paying for – our taxes are actually going to be paying for a bunch of people to fart around trying to find out 'what happens to us when we wait' for urgent treatment in a health centre. Stop! I'll tell you! Because, the next morning, I found myself hunched up in a chair in the doctor's surgery, trying to focus on an ant that was crawling up the wall by the flu jab poster to take my mind off the knives that were being thrust into my kidneys. Remember playing Ker-Plunk as a kid? Yeah, it was like *that*. I was praying to a God-I-don't-believe-in-anyway that my name would be called pretty damn soon because I'd been sat there for what seemed like hours and no one at all seemed to be going in or out, so the only way *'this experience can be different'* would be if the doctor came out and gave me some bloody medicine. I was most definitely *not* sitting there thinking 'Well, if I can just change my "internal space", I might not be feeling so shit.'

It's not that I have any objections to these places being brightened up, but what justification is there for spending what little resources the PCTs have on a few bits of 'art'? 'Art' isn't going to cure someone's kidney infection or enable them to be seen more quickly by a doctor. 'Art' isn't going to transform the life of some poor sod waiting seven hours in A&E to get their leg sewn back on. Whatever money the PCTs have MUST be spent on care. With the NHS in crisis, is it so unreasonable to question quite why 'culture' takes precedence over health? Taxpayers would prefer bug-free hospitals, an extra doctor here and there, and easier access to the treatment they require over a five-sided piece of yellow fibreglass with a poncy name standing next to the empty magazine rack by the toilets.

Parking my cynicism for a moment, let's look at this through the eyes of 2008's first out-of-town visitor to Liverpool, Capital of Culture. First thing to consider – how will they get here? If it's by plane, then it's obviously John Lennon Airport and, once outside the arrivals hall, it's a (very expensive) taxi or a bus journey into town where you can sit back and start getting excited about all the brilliantly creative things you're going to do while you're here – pretty hard to picture when you're having to drive through Garston and Speke. That's not being disrespectful to the residents of those areas, but, aesthetically (great word for 2008, by the way, *aesthetic*), it's hardly Pall Mall leading to Buckingham Palace is it? All this talk of 'regeneration' and nothing seems to have happened, at least not in some of the most important and needy places.

Some visitors might have done their homework enough to know that the #500 bus is the way to go. Straight into town, minimal stops and, if they're lucky, blacked-out windows from the *inside*. But it's inevitable that a significant number of people will be jumping onto any old bus that says 'Liverpool City Centre' on the front, which invariably means the 'Speke Express'. I'm not being funny, but I wouldn't imagine Eastern Boulevard to be a great first impression of a city you've never seen before, much less one proclaiming to be Capital of Culture. Ah, I know, culture has many faces, but the 'smacked arse' of Speke and Garston are faces you'd really want to save for last or, preferably, not at all.

It could be argued that decaying suburbs like these are part of our heritage, that it's where 'the street' is, where 'real' Liverpool resides.

Places like Huyton gave us Alan Bleasdale, Jimmy McGovern's from Everton (not his choice) and Halewood produced Jonathan Harvey. I'm not having a go at the people in the suburbs – most of us come from there – but they deserve more. I'm having a go at a council that thinks it acceptable to leave its own residents to rot while pouring millions into an already-rich city centre. If it wasn't for the people in postcodes L3–L100, Liverpool would never even have been considered a cultural ambassador to anything.

But back to the tourists, because they're the important ones here. Arriving by coach or car, well, there's a plethora of inbound routes to choose from. Lucky drivers. There's the East Lancs Road, East Prescot Road, the M62 and Edge Lane, Speke Boulevard, Crosby Road, the tunnels. Most of these arteries, like every major city's, pass through the suburbs but, with little exception, each of these roads will take you through miles of boarded-up housing, derelict warehouses, factories and neglected wasteground. It's a mournful sprawl. The 'Capital of Culture' seems only to encompass the city streets themselves. As long as Albert Dock is looking its best and there's room for three more Brazilian bars on Bold Street, that's OK. Doesn't anyone realize that by the time these visitors arrive in the city centre, they've already experienced 'culture' of a very different kind?

Some might insist that this doesn't matter, that the 'jewels' in Liverpool's (city centre) crown shine bright enough to extinguish the ugliness of what's outside it. Because Liverpool city is protected by an impenetrable golden halo of cash that stretches from Albert Dock, up to Hope Street, across to Paddy's Wigwam, over to St George's Hall and back to the Pier Head. Anything outside that Magic Square, forget it, you're not part of Liverpool. You don't exist. But unless they're going to issue blindfolds on all incoming flights, the backs of cabs and Arriva buses, there's going to be no avoiding the fact that Liverpool is much more than a renovated dockside and the Three Graces, because there are more *dis*graces that need attending to, urgently. Go to the Anglican Cathedral, then walk half a mile in any direction; you'll see poverty and isolation everywhere. Liverpool isn't any different from other cities in the UK in that respect, but isn't it a bit hypocritical to promote Liverpool as a capital of culture by ignoring the places that gave us that culture in the first place? As the saying goes, get your own house in order before inviting anyone inside.

One thing that *is* being taken care of, however, is the chronic accommodation shortage in the city centre. Apparently. There must be millions of rich people just waiting to move into Liverpool, but the developers are struggling to keep up with demand. The queues commuters face daily on the M6, M56 and M62 have nothing to do with rush-hour and roadworks, it's the thousands of removal vans pouring into the city each day depositing yet more people into Liverpool's swelling, pregnant metropolis. Isn't it? We've never been so popular! No sooner has one warehouse been converted than the cranes shift a few streets over to start on the next. Kerching! Surely we're going to run out of space to put all these people soon?! Or so the People in Charge would have us believe.

So it's with not a little shock that I learn that my own apartment, just outside the city limits, has fallen in value by £30,000 in the past three years, as a direct result of the epidemic of city-centre residential developments; developments that lie half-empty, that will *always* lie half-empty because there just aren't the people to live in them. I don't know the politics of who gives the go-ahead for urban projects like this and, to be frank, I don't care, as I'd bet whatever equity I have left that none of the decision makers actually live here. But how on earth can this level of development be justified? Where are all the people supposed to fill those apartments going to come from? Why is the green light being given to development upon development, when the majority of units are doomed to lie empty? I worked bloody hard for what I've got and, like most people lucky enough to be on the property ladder, my home is my security, my only real asset. Most nights for the past three years I've watched from my window above the city, as the cranes come and go, building hundreds upon hundreds of unwanted apartments, each new development knocking a few more grand off what my own place is worth, and there are thousands like me. It sounds bitter putting the words down but the simple fact is that Liverpool winning Capital of Culture is the one thing that might force me out of the city. I just cannot afford to live here any more and, if my property drops any further in value, I face a very real risk of bankruptcy.

Liverpool is supposed to be a city in the midst of a so-called 'regeneration' but, years into this scheme, there is little evidence of exactly what is being regenerated. I'm not talking about the multi-million pound Grosvenor Paradise Project (because Liverpool needs more shops…) or the permanent roadworks that masquerade under this 'Big Dig' banner like it's some kind of seaside fun day. As I write, it's November 2007. Does anyone *seriously* think all this disruption will have disappeared by January? That Edge Lane will look any different in two months? That the city is going to be anything other than one giant car park? With all the money being bandied about, you'd think the People in Charge would want to create a lasting first impression. They can bang on about the theatres and art galleries until the next millennium, but why doesn't anyone care about the urban hotbeds where, ironically, much of Liverpool's culture came from in the first place, and that still exists today? It's here, all around us, but it doesn't wear a black tie, live in a big house and lick arse, so there's no place for it.

The overriding 'USP' about Liverpool has always been the people here. It's a cliché already, and Liverpudlians are often accused of being over-sentimental about just how great we are, but it's true. We *are* great. And we're talented, without being arrogant about it, like Londoners. Musically, literally, comedically, I truly believe there isn't a place to touch us, but the Culture Company would rather bus in the 'internationally-renowned' and 'world-famous' than give a leg up to some of its own.

For example, Welsh artist Ben Johnson is aiming to complete his *Cityscape* project 'live' while resident at the Walker Art Gallery this spring. It's an ambitious representation of Liverpool's famous skyline and has been two years in the making, but, while there's no questioning Johnson's pedigree – he really is fantastic and has had several exhibitions in the city – shouldn't this project have been about finding a Liverpool artist to do the job? Staying with art, it is important to note that, at the time of writing, there is not one exhibition mentioned in the 2008 programme for the Walker and Tate that features a Liverpool artist. It's all 'international' this and 'world' that. Why? How many talented artists in this city must be frustrated that here was a golden opportunity for them to show off what they can do to a worldwide audience but instead the Culture Company chooses to bring in artists from elsewhere?

At the theatre, was I being unreasonable in expecting the Everyman and Playhouse to use 2008 as a way of introducing fresh, dangerous Liverpool writing? Obviously I was. I'm frustrated that, instead, these two esteemed establishments are 'playing safe' by putting on two productions that are determined to lock Liverpool in the past. Phil Wilmott's *Once Upon A Time At The Adelphi* (Liverpool Playhouse, July '08) is a musical comedy set in the thirties and Diane Samuels' *3 Sisters On Hope Street* (Everyman, Jan '08) is a spin on the Chekhov classic set in the Liverpool of the forties. I'm sure they'll both be successes and should be judged on their own merits, but wouldn't it have been a nice idea for the Everyman to do what it used to do best – contemporary, relevant social drama, showing us what's happening in Liverpool *today*? There are loads of local writers here crying out for a break, but the Culture Company just doesn't want to know. Even *Blood Brothers* is being resurrected for another run. Brilliant play, but everyone's seen it now and that slot could have provided an excellent springboard for something fresh and contemporary.

Musically, well it's the same old story. Paul and Ringo have been chauffeured in because, obviously, Liverpool can't celebrate anything cultural without them. Macca is 'very proud of the city' (which is why he lives in Sussex) and he looks 'forward to welcoming you all and showing you a good time'. Because, although Paul McCartney hasn't lived here for most of his life, he's still our leader and knows more about what's happening here than any of us who pay the council tax.

To be fair, it's probably not McCartney and Co. we should be criticizing, it's those who seem to think that no event in Liverpool can possibly be successful without the endorsement of an ex-Beatle or Ken Dodd, as though without them we are nothing. Well, there are only two Beatles left now, so what happens in twenty years' time when they're all gone? Another Big Dig, this time down the cemetery? Why do the People in Charge insist on keeping Liverpool trapped in the sixties? It's an honest legacy, no question, and something we should rightly be proud of, but 2008 should be about looking to the future, not living in the past. Liverpool has an exciting bunch of musicians and groups in the here and now, and we should be celebrating *them*.

When Liverpool won the culture bid and the fireworks went off in June 2003 I was thinking, great, at least there'll be a focus on Liverpool and people might actually start caring about the people in it, look a little closer, and realize that being creative doesn't have to mean knowing Shakespeare and talking posh. And this is where I'm going to contradict myself and say that our history *is* relevant, because there's a huge irony here. Why should Liverpool need to be 'designated' as a Capital of Culture? Hasn't it always been so? Every year we have festivals for comedy, music, theatre; we've never needed an official banner to parade under, we do it anyway. I won't list the dozens of names in all creative fields that have emanated from this city over the last fifty years, there isn't room. But it's a rich seam that is unparalleled anywhere else in Britain. We already have a thriving tourist trade thanks, in a large part, to this same creative heritage. Regeneration plans were already in place before the Culture bid was even considered. So why, exactly, did

Liverpool need this 'assignment'? Will it be like London 2012, a huge white elephant that the taxpayer ends up funding, whether they like it or not? Will it be a case of the politicians lining their own pockets, getting companies aboard this huge cash cow on whose committees they just happen to sit? What is Liverpool, Capital of Culture 2008, *for*? Well, it's for making other people rich, obviously. Apparently, between 2005 and 2007, the Liverpool Culture Company paid a London public affairs firm called FD-LLM over £300,000 from its funds to raise the profile of Liverpool among 'Westminster and Whitehall audiences'. What did they do? Buy them all a map of the UK with a big red pin stuck in it? Chuck a few LFC scarves around Parliament? £300,000?? Warren Bradley maintains that FD-LLM 'provided engagement between senior figures from the city and London-based politicians'. Which all works out as a very expensive jolly somewhere, probably The Ivy.

Question: Does anyone actually know who sits on the Liverpool Culture Company committee? Google it, go on, I dare you, because I bet you right now that no one who tries it will be able to come up with a definitive list of who does what and, if they're doing anything at all, how long they've been doing it. Harry Kewell spends more time on a football pitch than some of the Culture Company executives spend in office. The current committee (which will probably be a totally different committee by the time you've finished reading this) includes a former Director of Communications at the FA, an ex-Camelot director and a strategist who 'made his name in Australia'. It's like they're willing us to fail. I got a bit more excited when I saw Paul Newman was on board, but then quickly realized that it wasn't *that* Paul Newman. Shame. Is Phil Redmond still there? God knows. What *is* known is that the Liverpool Culture Company has a personnel turnover greater than McDonalds. They even employed a 'fixer' in October to be an 'extra pair of eyes to ensure the smooth running of the 2008 programme'. Bernice Law 'gets things done', apparently. So what's everyone else doing, then, if they need to employ someone just to 'get things done'?

Call me cynical, but let's not kid ourselves. While Liverpool as Capital of Culture will undoubtedly bring with it many memorable events and thousands more tourists to the city – whose money cannot be sniffed at – ultimately it's the People in Charge and their cabals who will benefit most. It's their job, not to look out for the interests of the people they represent, but to make themselves look good and make as much money as possible doing it. If we really want to be taken seriously as a capital of culture, then it's going to take more than a few over-priced bars and dignitary dinners to convince. Millions of pounds might well be injected into the 'city', but until people realize that the 'city' consists of more than the Albert Dock and the Radio City tower, it's the real Liverpudlians who'll be left wondering just what all the fuss was about.

2007

Taffy Scouse

John Jones

‑‑‑

My name is John Jones and I live in Rhyl, North Wales. I venture into Liverpool every second week to watch the boys in blue at Goodison. The reason I support Everton is because my father did and because my mother was born and raised in the Walton area of Liverpool. My dad told me of the history of the Welsh people who moved to Liverpool in their tens of thousands to build homes and settle on the hills at the top of Everton Valley. Welsh settlers built many of the terraced houses and streets in and around Liverpool city centre. There is even an area referred to as the Welsh streets in the south end of Liverpool. The Everton district of Liverpool became the main area for Welsh settlement in the eighteenth and nineteenth century and our namesake football team, the original on Merseyside I might add, became a Welshman's focus every Saturday at three o'clock.

Some of my fellow Welshmen have become famous at Goodison Park (Neville Southall, Gary Speed, Mickey Thomas, Dai Davies and Kevin Ratcliffe come to mind). Thousands of Evertonians reside in North Wales but I wonder how many of them are really tuned into the history of a fantastic city like Liverpool and just how involved Welsh people were in its building and formation.

My dad used to travel into Liverpool at the weekends to watch Everton in the daytime and Punk bands at night at the famous Eric's club. He reckons Liverpool people like my mum don't know how lucky they are, and that they take things like football, music and their heritage for granted. Where we live it is culturally dead! My dad won't be pleased to hear that but he knows it's true. He met my mum on one of his many weekend visits into Liverpool and was happy to find she was an Evertonian like him and her own mother. Her father, strangely, was a Liverpool fan and used to wind my dad up saying he didn't want his daughter mixing with some Taffy Evertonian, yet he had no problem letting my dad stay over most weekends once him and my mother were serious about each other. He's brilliant my grandfather, even though he's a red-neck! Anyway I'm going to be studying at Liverpool Uni soon and this was always the plan. Imagine my annoyance when the news broke about Everton FC moving to Kirkby. Part of my wanting to study at Liverpool was allied to my being able to get to all the games at Goodison. Kirkby is a Liverpool overspill and will not feel the same. My one hope for the Culture year is that Everton, like the Scousers my dad talks about, don't take their culture for granted by moving out into the suburbs. Everton belong in the city, where they are now, and that, alongside my dream of EFC UEFA Cup success, are my two big hopes for 2008.

2007

Paddy-Wack (Irish Scouse)

Paul O'Callaghan

—⚞⚟—

Travelling over to watch my beloved Liverpool FC nearly every weekend for donkeys, and from 101 bevvys I've enjoyed around the town in the last twenty years, I feel I've gotten to know this city well. Liverpool people have kept me up in house, shown me around the city, and basically acted like only the Scousers can. Although a lot of them have been politicized by their life within the city, and can be very opinionated to a point, I understand why some of them keep telling me that once and for all footballers' wages, match day admission, and Murdoch and Sky TV's exploitation of the game have gone way too obscene for them. Some lads I know have said they'd be acting completely phoney and going against their politics and principles if they carried on lining the pockets of agents, mercenary footballers and corporate moneymen.

Showing me how football culture has turned into pub culture for hundreds of fanatical people over the years, I wandered the Anfield boozers with some of them and they gave their reasons. The way they've been reared as football fanatics, it's something I can admire in a way; sort of like weaning yourself off a drug you've been hooked on for years. They didn't agree with me when I said supporting Liverpool FC was a worthwhile thing to do for the rest of your life, saying they would always want them to win, but financially and emotionally it's just not on with today's mercenaries.

I live in the Ballyfermot district of Dublin and travel over most weekends to stay in the city centre: the Radisson, Travelodge or the Marriott. Not wanting to fart about, let me tell you now: I live for my visits to the city of Liverpool. The people I meet here have given me open arms and open hearts, and for that I will be eternally grateful. Also, the football team has given me some of the greatest moments in my life. Sometimes Scousers come across as a bastardized version of Irishmen, in the way they tell stories, love to sing and dance and are warm and open-hearted. For me the place is a home from home, and wherever I travel in the world (as a computer consultant) I wear my small metal Liverbird with pride.

Whenever I travel over, either by plane to JLA or by sea ferry, I always have some sort of Liverpool book to pass the time. Because my travels have been extensive, without wanting to sound conceited, I reckon I know more about Liverpool's history than most Scousers do. I have made it my business. I know that it was often referred to as the capital of Ireland due to the mass exodus to the city during the 'famine years'. I also know of the great political trade unionist, Jim Larkin, who came from Liverpool to Dublin to galvanize working people in their struggle against British imperialism, and of Ireland's great footballers who starred for Liverpool and won medals galore: Ronnie Whelan, Ray Houghton, Steve Heighway, Mark Lawrenson, John Aldridge, Steve Staunton, Jim Beglin and Steve Finnan.

I am about to marry a Liverpool girl in Culture year and will be moving to the city after we're married. This was always my dream. To go and watch my team every weekend and to be 'in the know' concerning latest news and stuff is all I wished for; and nobody, I mean nobody could dampen down my enthusiasm for my home from home, my soon to be full-time place of residency. Funny, but I always knew I'd one day live in Liverpool.

2007

Scottish Scouse

Andrew McGregor

My name is Andrew McGregor, I am 29, single and work for a law firm; oh yeah, and I live in a brand spanking new Liverpool city centre apartment. I have lived in the city for four years and still haven't fallen out of love with the place I call home. Sometimes the scallies can do your head in, especially at the weekends when the place where I live (Slater Street) turns into something of a party zone. Sometimes the *Big Issue* sellers and druggies can be annoying. Sometimes the council services could be better and sometimes I wish the wind whipping up from the Mersey could be a little cooler as it blows onto my verandah. But, there you go, not many complaints.

Why I love living here. Passionate people. Passionate girls. Rocking nightlife. City on the up. Being Scottish, it doesn't feel like I live in an English city at all. For instance the other night almost the whole boozer was supporting Scotland against Italy in the football. I remember when I lived for two years in London (part of my law degree) and Scotland had two goals scored against them and everybody was cheering their bloody English heads off. I think with Liverpool it's a Celtic thing, and always sticking up for the underdog. Culture status is another good thing for the city, and the culinary delights at my disposal are now about as good as any single man could wish for (hence the trousers getting tighter). On my doorstep I have gyms, restaurants, theatres, shops and clubs, so, like I was saying, what more could a man wish for? OK, girls. Well I happen to think that Liverpool's ladies are not only stunningly beautiful, but are actually often quite mad, especially when it comes to partying, being up for a dare and having a giggle. They are often worse than the fellers for wanting to stay out all night (not arguing there, just that sometimes because I'm single they automatically assume that I'm up for partying all night). At the moment I would say that my life is a buzz and a bit of a breeze, and whenever I return to Edinburgh and my parents ask me 'No one in your life yet?' I think of all the friends I have (female and male) and think, no, no one serious at the moment... and long may it continue... Summing up living here, in what we sometimes refer to as the pool of life... plain and simple, in Scouse: life's deffo a proper buzz.

2008

English Scouse

Nicky Allt

All the citizens born and bred in Liverpool: how lucky they are
to be born here.

Scallies, Rag-arses and Meffs. Teds, Weirdos and Stormers.
Moaning Pensioners, Arl Sailors and smiling Biddies with piss-stained
drawers. Golf Balls, Beauts and Whoppers. Pop stars, Wannabes and
Models with orange gobs. Smackheads, Bizzies and Hot dog sellers.
Reds, Blues and Two be two's. Kopites, Gobshites and Not-rights.
Pyjama girls, Bobble hat Boys and Checked mint rocks. Jimmy One
Ball, Sandy Bramhall and Mr Cardboard Guitar. Anne Fowler's scary
women on Nethy Road, Toothless Brasses, and Spring Heel Jack.
Slobber chops, swallow the couch, and having an arse like Barney the
dinosaur. Hoffmans, leggers, and on one. Tramps who offer you out,
Designer Alky's in sound trainees, and Kick-off dogs. Bullrings,
Fontenoys and Four Squares. Gerard, Tommy White, and Caryl
Gardens. Tonking, Bonking, and Stonking victories. Jarg, Blowse and
Big Bad trainees. Minty, Custy and Boss trackies. Crusty Undies,
Grundies and Mad Mondees. Bag-off's, Cop-off's and Knob drop-off's.
Being Bevvied, Goosed, and Ruling the roost. Hoffman's, Igloo's and
Brasses. Meatheads, Grocks and Steg-heads. Inmans, Hoffmans and
Tasty scrans. Woollybacks, Sheepshaggers and Bad Blaggers. Arlarses,
Fruitcakes and Billy no mates. Cock of the school, Big Licks, and
Nobody's fool, Shitty arse, Mardi Gras and Shangrilas. Benders, Quegs
and Arse Bandits. Shady Blaggers, Shakehands McCarthy, and Plazzy
Gangsters. Boss suzzy's, School Buzzy's and Rushies Muzzy. Scotty,
Grotty and acting Snotty. Sausage and Mash, Dough and where's yer
Wedge. The Throstles, The Windsor and the Eagle and Child. Dot to
dot features, Map of Europe legs and Onion breath. Tool, Knob and
Bellend. Getting yer bare tit, Tom Tit and a Tiny little Stingy bit.
Inchy's perm, Reidy's hair dye, and Georgie Wood. He's in the Flock,
in me Pit and on the Nest. Judies, Birds and Tarts. Wheels, Mo mo's

and Bad Chariots. Bommy night, Crimbo and Making yer Communion. Proddy Dogs, Catlicks and Rag-heads. Vinny Two Bob, Johnny On Top, and Marty the Firebobby. Lends yer odds, Below the belt and Necking yer bird. Yer Nuts, yer Half and yer End away. King of the Kop, The Boys Pen, and Kemlyn Kneecap. Courting, Snorting and going to Moreton. Schoey's Lemmo, and Fishcake and Chips for Nosebag. Burnt cobs, Barmcakes and Scotts bread. Skipping the bus, leggers and Togger. Footy, Butty and Acting slutty. The States, yer Mates and Working lates. Graft, on Draft or getting a bad Waft. Snake in the grass, Scouse with red cabbage and Shitty Knickers. Going the Match, the Game, and having a Seaso. Ferries, over the Water, A bit of a Snorter, and have yer seen his Daughter. Burst out laughing, in Bulk and in Stitches. The Fung Loy, Rennie's and Capaldi's cafe. Deaf School, The Hoovers, and Blue Vein. Chips rolled up in boiled ham. Paddy's Market, The Ice Rink, and The Shewsy. Annabel's, Cindy's and the Livingstone. Having a Shite, the Turtle's Head and a Barry White. Kenny, Tocky and Fazak. Two Dogs, Sock Robbers and Crocky. Noggsy, Breck and Dodge City. Snorkels, Samba and Freds. Prada'd up, Armani'd up and Lacosted. Kecks, Rex and Kiting Cheques. Having a Mooch, On the Hoist and Chris Davies' Tailor made pockets. Snaggin', Laggin' Raggin' Shaggin' and Braggin'. Hichin' Bunkin' and Skyin'. Barney, Straightener and Offering you out. Greaty Market, Paddy's Market, and the Lanny. Brooky, Walton Ozzy and the Jirmins. The Chippy, Lippy, and a gob like Zippy. It's Nippy, Trippy and Mr Whippy. A 99'er, a 69'er and Digsy's Diner. Shack, Crack and going the Quack. On me Jack, Jeans are slack and Shake and Vac. Going off track, Taking Flack, and In the Nack. Strides, Snides and Teenage Brides. Tool, Fool and being a Mule. Railings, Peggies and Sugar Puff teeth. Derby Day Clashes, Nashers, and Sefton Park Flashers. Scary Kite, Lecky Lips and Twinkle toes. Disco Donny, Grab a Granny, and Graftin' inside the Grafton. Sausage Fingers, battered Swede and Elvis. Jelly Legs, Tatty head and a bad pair of Saggy Tits. Know the Score, Smart-arse and the Gangster Chronicles. Wearing a Johnny, Jumping off at Edge Hill and Ham-Shank. Mingebag, Doorhinge and Arl Scatter the Cash. Tight-Arse, Minge of the Month and No Dough. Muscles McCarthy, Mick McManus and Gigantor. Limey. The Betty, The Co-ee and going the Mo-ee. Hitler Muzzy, lost me buzzy and Toe-rag. Suedies, Gear and Ball Stranglers. Chewy, Spam and Sterry Milk. The Blue Star, Gianelli's chippy and the 051. Whispers, Litherland Town Hall and havin' a ball. Gordon Lee's Snorkel, Double-Click and Getting the

Special. Alpine Lemmo, Egg and Milks and 8 Walkers for a Penny. Mojo's, Beech Nuts and Lucky Bags. Lecky fiddle, Gas fiddle and Jimmy Riddle. Narky-Arse, Kick the bucket and Brown bread. Divvy, Skivvy and ice-cream mivvy. Twicer, Pineapple chunks and a forehead like a block of ice-cream. Monkey Boots, High leg Air Wair and Three star jumpers. Choppers, Chippers and Grifters. Bunkin' the Ferry, Rocky O'Rourke, and Scully. Oranjeboom, Breaker and Grolsch bottle tops. Flemings supatuff, Bakers and Seadogs. Fiorucci, Caio and Numan. Lois, Jesus and Kickers. Feather cuts, Wedges and Basin heads. Speedo's, Boxies and Catty's. Burst, A Wiss and a Sizzle. Street End, Park End and Road End. Kop, Knob on Flop, and Havin a Plop. Lucy's, Woodies and Embo. Jaffa Cakes, Pod and Trouser Snakes. Cheese on toast, Holy Ghost, and Racing Post. Roasties, Maccies and Lacky's. Joe Baxi's, Hurdy Gurdy's and Hairy Mary's. Havin a dump, On the lump and Havin a jump. Paraffin Lamp, Betty Stamp and a Fuckin' Tramp. Shitfaced, Twisted and Stella'd. The Big House, Ma Edgies and Ned Kelly's. Heebie Jeebies dancers, Primark girls, and The Girls who work in Next. Stanley Knives, Darts, and Golf Balls with nails in. Rusty Moggies, Sweaty Crevices and Spammies. The Tunnel Bus, Birkenheaders and Double-headers. Name yer pocket, at the Rocket and Rusty Barnets. Nudie Books, Dockers Hooks and Cook Da Books. China Crisis, Bunnymen and Icicle Works. Tates, Grates and Goin' the State. Maybes, Zutons and Corals. Skiddies, Bills and Sovereigns. Midget Gems, Cola Cubes and Swizzels. Subbuteo, Striker and Mousetrap. Arctic Roll, On the Dole, and The Yankee Pole. The Anorexic look, Parrot heads, and Plain old Bagheads. Big Issue Sellers who are Minted on the Sly. The The George, The Holt and The Leather Bottle. Jam Butty's, Ice Buns and havin' the runs. Sayers, Jacobs and Cream Crackered. Barry Bethel, White Riot and Cornies for Brekkie. Yokkers, Greenies, and Golly. Double-bubble, wearing ovees and working all hours. Cadge a lift, Hitchin' it and Getting' a Skipper. Bobby Charlton's barnet, Trevor Hockey's beard and Jack Charlton's neck. Mickey Finn, Bottle of Gin, and Listenin' in. Larks in the Parks, Do One, and On yer Bike. George Roper, Paulins Daniels and Sean Styles. Crusty nose, Picking crows and twiddlin' yer toes. Donkey Dick, Scabby Fanny, and a tremendous set of Zeppelins. Dog breath, Melt the Paint, and Sick Breath. Crap footballer, Bobby Dazzler and Dalglish on Toast. He's a Total Stallion, Wharra Man, and A bit of a Blurt. I'm only messin, D'yer wanna bet, and Do one Soft shite. Flemings, Air Wair, and Ben Shermans. Como's, Prince of Wales and

Bakers. Don't let-on, Who yer lookin' at, and kipper on im. Don't stick down, Show us the readies and Steady Eddies. Hairy plums, Sticky-out Gums, and stayin' in yer Mums. Go-ed La, robbin' a car, and I'm tellin' yer Ma. The Wizards Den, Blacklers Grotto, and The Punch and Judy. Giz a job, On the Blob, and Semi-lob. Margi Clarke, Violent Playground, and Platform 9 in Limey. Footy studs, Gammy leg and Not a Meg. Shoes like Pasties, A Collar to pick yer nose, and Beans on Toast face. A Gammy Leg, A Neckers Lip, and a neck like Gladstone Small. Wharra Blurt, Kirkby Kiss and Streak of Piss. T.J's, Erics the shop and All Mankind. The McGanns, Shankly and Harry Catterick. Irish jig, margarine fringe, and candy floss barnet. Johnny Gianelli's, the Lanny, and Ann Fowlers. Rigsby's cat, John Wayne's horse, and Paddy's market. Billy Fury, Ken Dodd and Jam Butties. Sterry milk, Being Shattered, and Ribs and footy on Boxing Day. Havin' a bash, spending cash and on the Lash. Gormless, Gorp and Gobshite. Lid, Kid, and Laaaad! Birds with Muzzies, fellers who wear suzzies, and Milfs and Huzzies. Round the twist, getting' pissed and Scotch Mist. The Derby, the National and Bommy night. The Bee Hive, Tiffany's and The Star and Garter. Catching crabs, Keeping Tabs and Hating Scabs. In the Bog, Chocolate Log and Wharra Dog. Play the Willy Banjo, Spin the Bottle and Off-ground Tick. Pair Knockout, 60 Seconds and Goalie on the Spot. Canny Farm, Back Bin and Jibbing in. Throwing Halfy's, Cups of Char and Gozzy Eyes. Lager Lout, Up the Spout and Robbing a Tout. Anne Twacky, Gabby Aggie and Chesty Morgan. Spring Roll fingers, Sui Mai balls, and a Khazi full of Fu Yung. Make-up kipper, Moose features and Arl Scare the Kids. The Yankee, The She and the Wooky Hollow. The State, Rotters, Baileys, Flintlocks, Tuxedo Junction, Checkmate, Scamps, Gatsby's, The Pez, The Night Owl, The Other Place and The Conti. Society, Mosquito and Garlands. Havin' a Toot, Show us the Loot, and D'yer think he's Fruit? Right, listen here Ginger-minge, Castle Grey-skull and Velvet Curtains fringe, I'm off, there's way too many; it goes on and on and on... alright! But while you're there, tell me which Liverpool sayings are named twice?

October 2007 ...
A Day in the Life

Nicky Allt

❦

Right, with my take on being a Scouser put to bed I'm gonna take you on a little walk with me accompanied by my un-English voice – the Liverpool one that feels as natural as breathing and as normal as a visit to the chippy after a decent bevvy. If the lingo gets a bit much then go and buy yourself one of those *Lern yerself Scouse* books. It won't help cos they're absolutely crap and well out of date, as Scouse language, like this city of ours, is forever changing. But at least you can throw it at the seagulls and pigeons who might try and steal yer chips. BANG! Let's go. Having had the misfortune to have lived most of my working life so far under the biggest and greediest bunch of lying Tory bastards you're ever likely to set eyes on, then the imitation Tories of Tony Eyebrows and new prime-minister, Rock of a Jock Brown (still a vast improvement on the first lot though), I find myself here today making a monumental decision to pack my spectator sport of choice (the footy) in for good. Might mean fuck all to you, but it's a move as big as Phil Thompson's nose for me. Thirty years down the line and my night-school re-education sees me seriously packing it in for good today. I've gone all opium for the masses on the footy, y'know with the Yanks taking over and building a new McDonalds spaceship for a ground and running things from couches in hot dog country. Yeah, it looks like a nice spaceship an' that like, but its American owned, which usually equates to another fuckin' supermarket where a loud kerching must always be heard above the Kop singing 'You'll Never Walk Alone' – dosh must be made eh brother!

It's another part of Liverpool culture which has been taken over and away from the masses by the bunch of bankers we call the moneymen. Thousands of fanatical supporters have already been priced out to the boozer, and some local pubs now resemble the Kop of old with the crowds they entertain when Liverpool kick off. Saying that, I wouldn't be surprised if the feller who agrees the ridiculous price hikes on match tickets owns or has shares in a local chain of boozers. I planned on 'going the game' till I couldn't walk any more. It's definitely not an age thing. See, my dream was I'd be 90 years of age and as the fifth goal got slotted against the Mancs, on the day we won the League for the 40th time, I'd keel over in joy and die of a footy-related heart attack in the Main Stand… perfect. So I repeat, it's definitely not an age thing. With players and their agents taking the piss and the club fleecing the supporters – the ones who made it famous and a worthwhile place to go in the first place – I just felt it flew in the face of the politics of my upbringing and of my Shankly-isms and I was being a phoney by keeping up my patronage. Me Evertonian mate, who knows where I'm coming from, and still thinks things are not being run right at Everton, says he's got to see another trophy before he jibs it. I'll still go if one of my kids asks, or the Saturday afternoon addiction overpowers me for a day, but now that there are so many things to write about and the fleecing that has always gone on becomes seriously obscene, never will I venture on that religious week-in week-out basis again.

I'm walking down Belmont Road in Anfield after passing my option for a new season ticket over to far younger and hungrier supporters. My hunger and direction are heading up different avenues these days as I try to make my way in the literary world. Oooer! Sounded all-lovey that. On a positive note: A world full of creatively inventive people who add colour, spice and entertainment to an often somewhat dreary existence. On a negative: A world full of Thespian Lesbians, Homosexual Has-beens and Forever Retro-Hetros, but a world I confess I always loved like Shankly and football till I met the story-robbing Has-beens side of things. Believe me when I tell you that when the small-minded, Southern-biased media lazily go on about the stereotypical Scouse thief, there are more story-lifters than shoplifters in Liverpool – miles more! Taking me away from literary thoughts for a moment, a pyjama-wearing teenage ma walks past. Her pram and swollen belly out front, her arse out back, reminding me of the arl swaying Kop in full 'Walk On' mode. For some mad reason her Arabian pyjamas let me know I should've done what I'm doing now ten years earlier, but I've been hanging the latch for a big fuck-off European Cup win – which we've recently carried off in the Bul – and another League Championship title to round things off and complete the full circle – which after Sunday's result against Arsenal is looking a long, long way off. But long may I be wrong.

Chip papers are swirling all over the road, getting caught up in pyjama pram wheels as I pass by a vandalized yellow speed camera. Two fat council workers struggle to try and fix it because the one at the top of the ladder, whose massive belly keeps shooting out over his kecks, is too busy laughing at pyjama girl's bucket of an arse as the camera keeps flashing on fast-as-fuck, ale-gut speed. I'm smiling, staring, while an ugly, hairy bellybutton stares right back at me. I give its owner a friendly wink towards pyjama cheeks. He gives a knowing smile right back. Coming down the ladder I realize he's Barney the Dinosaur in a yellow council coat. I'm making my way into town for a BBC radio interview about what makes Liverpool and its citizens tick and then I'll be making the most of Mad Monday and a bevvy in the Casa on Hope Street. I'm hoping the boozer never becomes truly successful otherwise the Yanks will undoubtedly put an offer in.

Walking on the opposite side of the road to the famous old Grafton ballrooms on West Derby Road, I think about the trillion and one Scousers who've strutted comos and stilettos on its dance floors while trying their best to cop off. Behind the Grafton lie the thousands of terraced houses they call Kensington. A far cry from its richer by billions London namesake, I don't think anyone's that arsed or even knows about the London version in this area. Many a bare-tit grapple has been smooched and wrestled on those small, carpeted living-room floors, after a night spent boogeying at the Grafton or Locarno. Edging down to Brougham Terrace, where successful smooches were lovingly sealed with a paper marriage certificate, it's got me wondering how many Liverpool marriages that started out in the Grafton were rubber-stamped here in heaven, and how many ended in tears, spears and oh my dears?

During the war thousands of foreign servicemen arrived at the Grafton in uniform to dance the night away. The place became known as 'the room of a million romances', as those servicemen became one of the first groups of non-locals to suss the illustrious charms of the Liverpool ladies. The iron-creased, Yankee-doodle-dandys were strangely offered the choice of legging it to the air raid shelter, or they could stay and carry on dancing and smooching whenever the Luftwaffe starting dropping bombs all around. Just imagine that, boogeying as the bombs drop. Many a GI bride met her gleaming, Donny Osmond smiling Yankee husband during those German air raids. I wonder if any unhappy marriages got the husband or wife thinking years later 'My God, I wish I'd have pissed off to the air raid shelter that night!' Maybe they were the first people to blame 'the Jirmins' for all their ills. It's got legendary status in Liverpool, the Grafton, same as its next-door neighbour, the Locarno ballroom and theatre (now the Olympia). Everybody has a tale to tell about these places, whether it was seeing the Beatles play in the sixties, meeting the wife in the seventies or grabbing-a-granny for a quick knee-trembler in a piss-stained back jigger in the eighties. People in Liverpool will always have a soft spot for the Grafton. It's been packed then empty, rich then poor, in and out of fashion, but remains forever there like a Scouse copulation trademark, a Beacon of Bonk! It's real Liverpool, with knobs on and knobs out. I would bet good money on stating that the back alley behind the club has seen more five-knuckle shuffles than the busiest casino in Las Vegas.

After shuffling past the fate-sealing, confetti-paved Brougham Terrace we're in Nowheresville, as a planners' blight on the edge of town splits Kenny from the city centre. It was here many moons ago after one of my first visits to the Grafton that I had to literally fight my way off a coach full of rampant St Helens women. Dressed to kill and out on a hen party with sex and laughter on the brain, I'd been speaking to one of them earlier in the evening of a normal Saturday night out – a devil's dare from one of my mates. Come lashing out time, and after a serious good laugh with the St Helens scrum down, we told them we'd like to jump aboard. Sandra, the woman I was speaking to, told me she was forty. She laughed like Red Rum after its third National victory when I told her if that was so she must've had her face in the oven on a low light, because she looked nearer the big five-o all day and all night to me. Put it this way, she wasn't offended. A woman on 'lad for the night patrol' never is. I was eighteen. My co-boarding buddy, Tony, nineteen. Both of us were game-as-fuck for anything on offer.

Now these St Helens girls had bee-lined us inside the club, ushering us upstairs to the fondle suite where, truth be known, we were easily and happily ushered to. With bums and bosoms having neon-lettered tattoos that shouted 'lift me out quick', Tony was sat between two of them in seconds. Cheese in the cheese sarny, it was as though they were willing to have a half young Scouser each for the night. And young Tobo, blubber lips on speed, was red-cheeked, trouser peaked and absolutely loving the attention! Meanwhile, dirty big Sandra was busy getting me into a half-nelson before one of her shy retiring mates beat her to the ciggy-burnt casting couch. It looked like I'd already got the part of lad for the night when I was instantly lip-locked by Sandra, who from memory had a strong resemblance to Joan Rivers when the Yankette was only one facelift in. Sat lapping at my gob like a self-squirting, shoe polishing machine, I dropped an eye to the right to view Tobo already starring in 'Confessions of a kid who's dying for it!' We had a good half-hour on those casting couches till we all agreed it was time to return downstairs to the Saturday Night Fever dance floor.

Once two o'clock chimed in with a few 'Me and Mrs Jones' type slowies me and Tobo noticed the girls heaving and hovering in the aisles. Thinking it would be a laugh to be smothered in tits, bums and tattoos, or looking at it cynically, ink-tagged middle-aged lard, we sneaked onto the coach as the driver, head in a cloud, tried to remove mortar with his willy against a wall. Thirty minutes later we were diving out the fire escape door with undies around ankles not knowing whether to laugh, cry or head straight for Rex Makin's offices to file a claim under 'Bus ravaged'. Suppose it's one thing meeting those St Helens ladies on a level playing field where a lad stands an outside chance of dodging a flying rugby tackle, but on the backseat of a tattered charabanc with not an inch for a body swerve we stood no chance. Diving out on this same eyesore of an industrial estate we eventually got a taxi to stop, before laughing our heads off all the way home about how we'd been gang-raped by those rugby-playing, woollyback mad women. Laughing again, years later, we reckoned it was the closest we'd ever come to being Chippendales for a night. Sadly, after three more pints we agreed we were now 'chip and ale' men every night.

Down the nonentity that is Islington (Drizzlington – it's about as dreary as Liverpool gets), past the ugly trade union building that doubles up as Liverpool's biggest khazi every Saturday night – deservedly so – just before taking the cut through to the centre of town, I hit my first glorious stop. Quick double-take, I cross the busy thoroughfare and drift back in time as the grandeur of my favourite Liverpool street and view comes fully into focus. After walking down Islington it's as though you've just stepped out the back of the wardrobe from the Lion and the Witch story. Slipping onto the cobblestone sidewalk fronting the old County Sessions house, the timeless Walker Art Gallery and the Picton Library tell you you've left the wardrobe behind and entered Liverpool's Oliver Twist scene. Across the cobbles stands the Steble Fountain, the Wellington Monument and the city's crowning glory, the beautiful St George's Hall. Designed by 23-year-old Harvey Lonsdale Elmes, who, overworked and unwell, died not long after, it's one of the finest buildings in England. Thinking about poor Harvey, I wonder if he'd found better health and lived on he'd have topped the design of this place? I can't help but think some more: what an achievement for one so young. As I always do on view, I linger to breathe it all in… What an absolutely stunning gaff!

A host of old scenes from my past and Liverpool's past instantly cloud my thoughts. I go through the same double-take every time I tread the cobbles of William Brown Street. It's a place that sends shivers down my spine. A ghostly wind adds to the feeling as I stand in the place where a famous old photo was first taken of some poor, young, raggedy-arsed street urchins sat smiling, barefoot at the base of the fountain a hundred years ago. I clock my own wheels and realize I'm brewsted in comparison. I remember Bill Shankly speaking to the crowd here after the 1974 FA Cup Final when he said Chairman Mao had never seen such a show of red strength. An inspirational man put into an inspirational scene. Inspiring indeed! While he spoke from the library balcony I clung to a lamppost in my baby Air Wair, utterly mesmerized by the Scottish messiah. Lodged in my memory box it never fails to add bounce to my stride. Even the Evertonians liked Shankly.

On Sundays, visiting my Nana and Grandad's home on the top floor of Gerard Gardens tenements, which used to back onto the museum and art gallery, I'd often saunter over just to breathe in the aura of the place. Timeless with beauty and, surprisingly, still unspoilt by the city's idiotic planners, it feels no different thirty years on. It's one of the only places from memory that still feels untouched. I got told my first joke here. Well… the first joke I can remember. I think the surroundings jammed it in my memory box so vividly. It was a sunny, Sunday afternoon – it's nearly always sunny in my memory for whatever reason – sat at the side of the fountain I eyed another young kid. Younger than me, he noticed me noticing, beckoning me over with a regulation stick in his hand (again from memory, always sticks?) Child-like and unwary I wandered over. The rogues and scallies of the day roamed in gangs, but this kid, toothless grin, wild hair, shirt and v-neck jumper, looked harmless and friendly – bit like a street-suss Bamber Gascoigne. Like most young Liverpool kids I already had my built-in scally-radar. The fact that it was finely tuned and this lad emitted no red warning signs or flashes sent me over. He shouted to me from one side of the fountain. 'Did y'hear about the little Liverpool kid who lifted a load of sweets from a London Road newsagents shop, an' kept eatin' all the

Cadbury's chocolate bars sittin' here on the fountain?'

'No' I firmly stated, trying to look tough, nodding side to side as I spoke.

'Ee-ar mate, sit here.'

Friendly alright, I'm thinking, making my way around the cast iron perimeter.

'Well after eatin' five he was just about to eat his sixth, when an' arl gentlemen sat on a bench over there started shakin' his head, shouting: Son, eatin' all that chocolate's bad for yer. It'll give yer' acne, rot y'teeth an' make y'fat!'

Drawing me in as he spoke, I'm nodding along.

'So the little kid shouts to the arl feller: Ah forget all that, my Grandad lived to be 107. So the arl feller shouted back: But did y'Grandad eat six bars of chocolate at a time? An' the kid looked at him an' said: No, he just minded his own fuckin' business!'

Laughing out loud, I stopped abruptly when I clocked him eyeing me head to toe. For a moment I began to think the joke was a piss-take, all because for fleeting seconds we'd locked urchin stares and, growing up in Liverpool, that was the quickest way to find a fight. Suddenly he burst out laughing at my laughing and regaled me with more tales of Liverpolitania. So a new Sunday-only friendship was made.

A lot of Liverpool meetings and greetings are like that. Like scenes from a comedy play where humour is used in the opening lines. And with the humour being cruel, cutting and abrasive, if you're fat, skinny or hairy, then you're the fattest, skinniest or hairiest person on the planet... according to your mates. For full Scouse effect, treble the above statement by three. Outsiders simply don't get it! This can be the cause of many a stern word, misunderstanding, or downright straightener. For instance, with the play I co-wrote, *Brick up the Mersey Tunnels,* a well-known stage director was brought from London for the first script-in-hand reading. After meetings and greetings were exchanged the director sat comfortably in her pretend deck-chair to have a quick shufti at the script. After a while she lifted her director's cap to say that the first thing she noticed was that the dialogue and jokes were a little too abrasive and could the writers tone it down a little? Needless to say she travelled back to London through no fault of her own, other than the fact that typical Liverpool humour touched a different type of chuckle button than the one she was used to. In truth, she was probably a London grad student, migrated in from some Southern backwater, because those inner-city born and bred Londoners, like the old Eastenders for instance, had a lot in common with your born and bred Scouser. We eventually found the right director and the rest as they say is local theatrical history.

If you begin to understand Liverpool street theatre and the pavement patter and Mersey mannerisms, and you can embrace the best of them and feel comfortable around them, then you are on your way to becoming an honorary Scouser. This is not a title bestowed flippantly, and a thousand closed-minded, stiff-upper-lip types have been left floundering in the Mersey willing their degree years at Liverpool Uni to finish quick-as, as they struggled with getting an angle on Liverpool life. Good thing is, a lot more Uni students are calling this home for life and staying here and putting down roots. A new phenomenon hardly heard of till recent times, it's a reversal in graduate departures that tells a good story all by itself. Face it, it can only be good for the city when the academically inclined are starting to learn the lingo, adapt, settle and bring their own bats to the brainy ball game. Long may they live and learn in Liverpool, I say.

At the moment I'm taking a book back to the library that I've just read in a day. It's a neat little book called *Gateway to the Empire*, written by an ex-sailor called Tony Lane. Tony was a Southerner from the Isle of Wight who came to live here after first feeling the warmth of the city people on returning from Australia following his first overseas voyage. You can find the book in the local section of the Picton library and these are Tony's words about why he stopped in Liverpool. 'I found Liverpool a warm and welcoming place. I loved the city streets which opened to the River and the brass plates announcing ocean connections. I loved the blunt self-confidence of the people who would claim a stranger as a fellow member of the human race. I loved the anarchic, good-humoured mockery of a people who refused to be servile and defiantly guarded their independence. I think I quickly noticed this social character that has made Liverpool such a decidedly distinctive place, but thirty years ago [when he first stopped here] I was far too young and ignorant to begin to understand what had formed the city and its people. I knew only that I felt more at home here than anywhere else I had ever been.' And there you go, well in Tony, I couldn't have put it better myself. So to those students of business and law and all forms of scholastic pursuit who are contemplating putting down roots here in Liverpool 2008, I say, welcome. You have come to the right city to learn all about life, so allied to your academic studies, I say, yeah, welcome again my learned friends.

Carrying on my walk I cut into St John's Gardens, where I can see the huge mousehole that the Wirralians escape through every night after taking their Cheshire cheese from Liverpool's larder. Another great source of Scouse separatist humour from Liverpool jokelore is just how touchy some people from the dark side can be. The snootiest of them (Heswall and Hoylake's finest) send letters to the local paper crying about the uncouth Scouse accent, the scallies in the streets and the rising price of tunnel tolls. At the moment it's one pound forty each way to cross the Mersey by car through the tunnel, and I don't know why they are moaning. The true price should be two pound eighty when crossing from the Wirral to Liverpool, as thousands do each day, and zilch crossing from Liverpool to the Wirral as everything of note lies this side of the water: the history, the culture, jobs, yada yada yada. Birkenhead apart, the Wirral is quiet and leafy and a nice place to go to sleep, and... that's it. No Liverpool, no Everton, no Grand National, Beatles, nightlife... humour?

See, I'm going on a bit now – like Liverpool's list of favourite sons, daughters and historical happenings does, and having a bit of banter – like Liverpool does. That's all. In truth, it's a lovely place the Wirral... to go to sleep. And we might as well trumpet and go on because, face it, no one else will for us, and we might as well joke and take the mickey because no one can quite like us. When I mentioned the word unequivocally in my support of *almost* all things Scouse, I use the word *almost*, as every now and again, like it sometimes does for Southerners, central government and other outsiders, there are things about the place that can become a right pain in the bum-hole for reasons I'll explain quickly and briefly.

One of the things that pure does my head in is the litter, shit and debris the council think we're all happy to live with in our streets (it's a Wirral letter this one). When are they going to employ an army of people to sweep and clean the ollers, alleys and thoroughfares once and for all? Liverpool people pay one of the highest council taxes in the country, yet it's like they only see the city centre when it comes to a decent hose down. Salary cut for the highest earners equals cleaner streets, maybe? Not a chance Pedro! Not including local opinion in the general planning of major city renewal and construction is another serial annoyance, and same as or similar to the non-collab-oration with local communities when considering the Culture year celebrations. They dangle regeneration carrots that say we'll fix up your house and the area where you live, but don't get involved or it might delay the process, so we'll employ our own faces and we'll do the job and spend the megabucks as we see fit. It reminds me of the middle and upper-classes who own and run publishing firms who tell you they'll publish your story only if you tell it the way they see fit. The non-participation and ignoring of locals is almost as bad as the one that comes top of the tree for letting Liverpool down and holding us back year after year, and that is: local government and council in-fighting. The three things above are all to do with politics and politicians, and while they constantly in-fight and see no further than the end of their own noses and bank balances, then all's we can expect is continued mediocrity. They can be summarized as: Bigger budget for a cleaner environment due to more money at hand from savings made from obscene salaries. People being allowed to participate in their own regeneration, leaving a better sense of community after the works are complete. And finally, no more in-fighting, how long do we have to shout that old nugget?

Meanwhile local councils and politicians of other places out-fight, not in-fight, for the greater good of their respective cities, thus creating a better life for the inhabitants they represent. If anything is or has been 'badly wrong' in Liverpool life over the last thirty or forty years, it has been the wasted decades of in-fighting. Simply put: it holds us up and holds us back, while other less talented cities basically get on with doing things for the betterment. Who knows, maybe it's part of the belligerent, confrontational nature of the people that they end up wasting so much energy arguing and fighting with each other? Seems that way sometimes, till you see the bigger picture and realize it's a case of 'jobs for the boys', 'I'll scratch your back' and finally 'nobody being held accountable'. As for the heavier criticism of the city, that, my friend, is about it.

You'll have noticed I haven't got a lot of time for complaining about or sending the boot into Liverpool as there are enough high-profile people and London and Manchester-based media to do all that for us. After a bout of Liverpool jokes took newspaper centre stage some years ago (What d'yer call a Scouser in a car? – getaway driver, Scouser in a suit? – the Accused, Scouse girl in a white Lacoste trackie? – the bride; I smiled at that one to be honest) it took a great writer like Bill Bryson to visit the place and redress the balance: 'The factories may be gone, there may be no work, the city may be pathetically dependent on football for its sense of destiny, but the Liverpudlians still have character and initiative, and they don't bother you with preposterous ambitions to win the bid for the next Olympics.' It takes an honest outsider who has travelled about a bit to give a truer slant on things. With our neighbouring city of Manchester it's definitely a case of familiarity breeding contempt, as they'd claim to love us, and probably would, if we were based thousands of miles away and they were not in our cultural shadow any more. True, they've had a bit of a go the last twenty years, but tell me about the larger than life Mancunians that the rest of the country knows all about. I'm not trying to score brownie points here, but it deffo irks them.

Face it, there's always a new Scouser-phobic waiting to have a pop isn't there? In recent years I can recall Anne 'face like a tea-strainer' Robinson (the 1966 Alan-Ball-ringer of the TV presenting world) yeah, I'm taking it out on her again, as old dot-to-dot kipper had to take it out on Liverpool for being called mousey in her old Crosby school days didn't she? Either that, or she got chucked by her first boyfriend for having no lips and she's still not over it. As did Boris 'Banana' Johnson (a gormless, public-school wank veteran with nothing better to do than jump on the Scouser-phobic bandwagon); and Alan Bennett (it simply made a change from writing about his schoolboy fantasies); and that miserable, ugly beaut with the sideboards and Victorian clobber who does the horse racing on TV, John 'Tweed Knob' McCririck. Give him his due though, he had some front having a go at Scousers the way he speaks and looks. And how could I forget Kelvin 'verbal diarrhoea' McKenzie, of *Sun* newspaper infamy, who wanted to impress his bosses by selling lots of newspapers after the 1989 Hillsborough disaster, so came up with his pathetic 'robbing and pissing on the dead' headline concerning the terrible tragedy. Anything to kiss the boss's arse and score a few 'Brown-eye' points eh Kelvin? He still hasn't admitted his filthy lie, or apologized, but he will one day – if he's man enough. And while I'm there, what's your culture about fruitcake?

Continuing up through Whitechapel I think of Jack Sharpe's sports shop where I used to get a football kit every Christmas: an Umbro box with socks, shorts and a jersey inside. My ma would take me and my two brothers there early December, religiously, and how we buzzed when we knew she'd bought those Umbro specials. Liverpool red used to end up with a pink collar after a few washes, while Everton blue had a sky blue collar come New Year. The field where I lived would be full of kids in pink and sky blue collars in January, unless you were a trendy footballer who wanted the new Crystal Palace vertical stripes, the yellow and sky-blue of Brazil, or the green and black striped Coventry away. The paying parents and the wearing kids just wouldn't put up with those discoloured vicar-type collars nowadays.

In the same block where Jack Sharpe's once stood lies the Culture Company shop. It cost a fortune to set up, sells souvenirs for 2008, and has fancy pamphlets and books that hardly anybody in the city knows exist. Walking through its doors I pick up a leaflet stating something about 'The World in one City'. Now let's have this straight. Liverpool today is one of the least culturally diverse cities in the country. We used to be the most culturally diverse, but large migration to Liverpool stopped years ago. The leaflet is talking bollocks and should read 'The World in one Person', because most native-born Liverpudlians have blood from all corners running around inside their bodies. At the last double-quick count I had Irish, Italian, Norwegian, Spanish and German blood and ancestry as part of my DNA make-up. The majority of your native-born Scousers have 'The World in one Person' not the city like the dodgy pamphlet says.

A small poster on the wall tells the story, advertising my next play *A Tale of Two Chippies*. I know it's mine from a distance because I stuck it there. Only time will tell if it's going to be decently received in my hometown, and people keep asking me 'Will it travel?' And I honestly answer, 'I couldn't give a shite as long as people in Liverpool like it!' Thinking of hunger and thinking of chips I'm tempted to aim for the Lobster Pot where, like my brethren, I've ended up on hundreds of occasions at throwing out time. But the smell of Scouse comes drifting through the air from a side street café, and as it's winter and my ribs are in shiver-me-timbers mode, I'm thinking, *nothing defrosts like a good bowl of Scouse* – nothing! It's the one beef and vegetable stew that will always reach the parts that other dishes cannot reach.

This city centre should be called Reminder Town for people like me, as every place I walk past or go into has potential to send me to into reverie on visitation. With the fantastic aroma of Scouse pervading the air I enter the café to place my order: Scouse, red cabbage, crusty bread and a bottle of Vimto – get paid! Same scoff as J.M. the councillor from past pages. Sitting down, I think of the old Liverpool joke where Jimmy Riley goes into a Liverpool doctor's and says, 'Doctor, Doctor, with it being the winter, I'm addicted to Scouse and red cabbage. I've been eating five bowls a day and can't stop!'

'There's nothing wrong with that sir', replies Doctor Johnson.

'But Doctor, I know it's good for you, but I can't stop shitting chips! Me Missus says it must be all the spuds I'm eating.'

'OK, pants down… bend over, I'll examine you', says Doc Johnno.

Jimmy bends over, and after a bit of humming and harring the doctor says, 'Carry on with the Scouse Mr Riley; it's the greatest food on earth at this time of year. Come see me in a few days if it hasn't cleared up.'

Jimmy returned to the doctor's a week later. 'Doc, you're a genius. I'm still on the Scouse and I've stopped shitting chips. What did yer do?'

'I cut eight inches off yer string vest that's all!'

It's an old Liverpool joke but one that has stayed with me since I was first told it as a little kid, bit like the chocolate one. The opening monologue of a play I wrote, *A Tale of Two Chippies*, now showing at the theatre, about a shop that sells Liverpool's staple diet, tells one woman's story of life in 2008. Set against a backdrop of ancestral emigration to today's Capital of Culture, the main protagonist is the imaginary Linda Gianelli. The Gianellis were a real Liverpool family from the city's Little Italy community, based around Gerard Street. They owned what was probably the finest fish and chip shop in Liverpool, if not famous for its fish then definitely for its chips. The play, a comedy, tells of how a Liverpool woman who lost her husband some five years ago is now threatened with the closure of her livelihood (a chip shop) when the council send her a compulsory purchase order due to the 'Big Dig', and because corporate chip shop, Harry Ramsden's, is about to take over the street. It's all about what unfolds as Culture year kicks in: red carpet treatment if you're down as outside investment; shown the back door if you're local and been here for years. Written to coincide with the Cultural celebrations it ends on a happy note with Linda finding a new husband and a new chip shop – all say ah.

Set in modern-day Liverpool, it starts like this.

Linda stands at the counter area, cleaning and preparing food.

LINDA: They're a suspicious lot round here. But, y'know, y'can't really blame them. I mean, take this Capital of Culture lark. First we win it cos of the people of Liverpool, but once the decent jobs come ridin' in who do they stick on the horses? Yeah, the likes of y'Robin bleedin Archers and y'Jason bleedin Harborows. I mean, God, you'd think we were all friggin' useless wouldn't yer. Take my Grandad for instance; he came here from Genoa, Italy, with

nothin' but a recipe, a small bag of tools an' some pearls of garlic
to ward off any sea sickness – an' any saucy sailors (limp wrist),
he'd joke…Yeah, one of the League of Nations Grandad Gianni,
but, no ridin' in on any gravy train for him… No, he was one of
the millions who saw the Pierhead and stayed put, especially after
crossing that bears-arse of a sea over there. (Pause)
Ooh… give me a sec…

She shuffles chips, adjusts temp. Generally getting things ready for
evening business

I have to give them a bit of a shake see (laughs) an' once they start
cookin'an' bubblin' the fat always reminds me of the Mersey to-in'
and froin'. An' I'll tell y'what, talkin' of rough sea an' where me
Grandad jumped ship, it's our very own Ellis Island that Pierhead
landin' stage… isn't it! An' with all the shite this place has been
through it's a wonder there's any landin' stage or city left an'
that we haven't all been swept away into the Irish Sea for good.
I mean, (Phew pause) it's been flattened by Hitler till there was
nowhere left to flatten, bled an' fled from by Slave Traders an' rich
merchants till there was nowhere left to bleed, an' stabbed in the
back by Politicians an' media types carryin' pens that coulda made
excalibur look like me Grandads spud peeler. Ha – suspicious, god,
y'not bleedin' kiddin! See… you walk the streets of this city tryin'
to spread some good news, they'll say: 'Nah, round here; can't see
it meself girl. It'll never happen.' You walk those same streets an'
try' n' tell them the bad news, an' they'll offer: 'Nah, don't worry
Linda, it'll all be alright, you'll see'. Y'can't win. Y'might as well act
the Warren friggin' Bradley an' tell them Whatever they wanna
hear… Scuse me a sec, let me just sort these pies.

Linda puts pies in the oven and checks food then her appearance
in a mirror.

(Fixing hair) Gotta try an' conform to what a decent cook looks like
haven't yer'… An' face it we've never really been the conformin'
type have we? I mean, look at John Lennon… Bessie Braddock…
Jack Jones… most of our heroes were never what you'd call
the conformin' type were they? Well, were they? Since I was in
uniform an' white socks me Grandad had taught me all about our

cantankerous bloody history. By the time I passed me eleven plus an' went to SFX, I was ready to blow up the houses of bleedin' Parliament in search of some honest-to-god-truth! An' that's our problem isn't it – we just don't suffer fools enough do we – too in y'face, that's Liverpool's problem. But talkin' of faces we were always welcomin' to new ones weren't we? Immigrant city see. Ah, suppose people don't open their hearts as easily today – more guarded – for that an' a couple of other reasons I almost moved on meself, but me Grandad wanted me to finish off what he started here… I know that now. Anyway, with all the tonnage these docks have swallowed it's only my opinion, an'… I'm just a small crispy in a portion of those (points to chips). An' move! Move to where? We were eventually gonna move this place nearer to London Road, back where Grandad started it all. Then this bleedin' council gave warnin' that a compulsory purchase order might be in order, statin' it might be part of the big dig. Yeah, well the only big dig round here'll be me diggin' me bleedin' heels in cos they can friggin' well sod off! If I have anythin' to do with it – an' as usual, I probably wont – I'll go when I decide, not when some stuffed shirt tells me to. Anyway, the ol' place is startin' to look a bit dapper these days, especially since this phony Culture thing finally got its brush an' shovel out. (Pause) Thing is, if you look long enough among the Docks in any Sailortown you'll find between the Scallywags, rebel rousers an' nonconformists plenty of bruised an' beaten hearts of gold. I found one some years ago an', as the sayin' goes, God, 'He was a cracker'. Me own fella with the golden heart: My Frankie. Sure as that river (points) flows out past New Brighton point before rushin' back on breakers full of sand, y'could guarantee a story an' a welcomin' smile from that one! (laughs) God, I miss y'Frankie (heaven) like me Grandad you were a cracker alright!

Telling it in local dialogue, I tried to paint the picture of an entrepreneurial Scouse woman who loves and respects her city, but whose ruling fathers don't love and respect her. Anyway, as I've said, the main reason I'm in town today is I've been asked to be part of a BBC Radio presentation about the culture of Liverpool and I'm meeting the producers, Gavin Whitfield and Neil McCarthy, at Paddy's Wigwam to discuss all things local, all things Scouse. The two have just contacted me by mobile to say they'll be waiting on the steps of the cathedral as they want a decent skyline panorama for an interview. Because I usually get up at five o'clock in the morning to write, come midday I'm normally finished for the day, so wanting a bevvy after abstaining at the weekend, I'll jump a Joe up to Hope Street, and interview finito, I'm on one to the Casa to let another mad Monday begin.

Before I cross town I venture over to Wetherspoons near Mathew Street, right opposite where Probe Records used to be. I vision the peacocks like Courtney Love, Pete Burns and Jayne Casey who used to hang out here back in the day. God, how safe does everyone dress compared to those late seventies Punk days? Safe is the way now. Got to fit in, not stand out. I've got to drop some flyers for the play…

Sat inside having lunch are two safe-type young lads I know, Darren, 21, and Tommy, 20, who immediately greet and tell me they are on something of a monstrous mission. They first tell me of calling in at the Culture Shop where they were thinking of volunteering as cultural ambassadors. They reckoned it might have been a great way to meet tasty foreign girls who they would have had to guide around the city as part of the job. Once they found out there was no pay involved, not even expenses, they wrote it off as a mug's game. Half-talented footballers in their schooldays, they've found the pro-footballer blag gets them all the kudos and girls they need. Both lads earn good money so flashing the cash is no problem. With self-employed plumber Darren still living at home with his mum, and Tommy keeping his finger on the pulse by having a flat in town and a small designer clothes shop and market stall of his own, the two have found that if they keep it tight they can carry out the deception all the way to the bed covers. Unless, that is, they meet a girl with the inquisitive mind of a lady detective, or somebody who's heard all about their little night-time ruse.

By telling the ladies they're youth team players with Glasgow Celtic (north of the Border deemed safe so nobody finds out, and team can be changeable), they think they're onto a winner. But they've been caught out before. Like the time a girl they tried to reel in asked Darren his religion. Replying Catholic, she further enquired if it had been a problem signing for Rangers, like it used to be in the old days. Thinking Tommy had changed to Rangers for the night, he replied the religion thing was no longer an issue and Rangers had signed him up in a flash. She laughed, calling him an idiot seeing as Tommy had said they both played for Aberdeen. Changing tack, he quickly changed teams to Aberdeen, only for her to reply that he was an even bigger fool. His mate had said they played for Celtic. Never mind. To Darren and Tommy it's all part of the game, you know, you win some you lose some.

With wannabe Wags all over town (their words) trying to find a fast track to the fame game, a collision with the two wannabe footballers, who think anyone and everyone is fair game, is imminent for at least some of them. And, after all, isn't that what their parents have told them, that 'life is just a game'. Winners, losers and who gets hurt, aren't they just the consequences of rolling the dice and taking part? Darren tells me he's going to work in Australia soon; he says he's always fancied living somewhere else for a few years, but definitely nowhere else in England. Tommy interrupts, telling him he's a fool, that he's earning good money and Liverpool girls are the best laugh and best looking. The two are typical 'couldn't care less' young lads, dressed smart and looking the part, out for a good time and not wanting to think about the consequences of what they're doing at all. They ask me about the flyers and when I say it's a play I'm putting on they tell me almost in unison, 'A play, the theatre, ah, I don't go there'. I try telling them what it's about, but give in quickly when I see no light shining in their eyes. Tommy says he enjoyed *The Boys from the Mersey*, my little attempt at a footy story, and likes reading football books (Steven Gerrard's book lies on the food table) so I tell them they should read Paul Du Noyer's *Liverpool: Wondrous Place*, or Robert Tressell's *Ragged Trousered Philanthropists*. Bidding my farewells, the two of them look like they're already on a Wag hunt. I'm off.

The two lads from BBC Radio are stood atop the steps. Climbing the Catholic stairway to heaven I take in the view. Cranes and new buildings litter the skyline. You come back here in five years it'll be changing again. A microphone is thrust in front of me, as Gavin, the show's producer, asks me, 'Well, what do you think of the view?'

'It's Liverpool isn't it.'

'Of course it is, where else would it be?' He answers.

'It couldn't be anywhere else' I reply. 'I can smell the sea up here, it's Liverpool.'

Another moment of reverie kicks in. Noticing, he leaves me be as I suck it all in. The only thing still free around here: Liverpool oxygen with that Mersey twist. But it's special stuff you know. There's definitely something in the Liverpool air. Could 2008 and the regeneration of the city herald a bright new dawn, or another false one? We've seen enough of those. The building work tells me things are happening, but it takes more than bricks and mortar. Then I think about all the things that have made Liverpool truly great; the human things. All those ambitions and ideas that started out in Mary Ellen's loins, or as a small acorn that one man or woman planted, dreamed about and saw all the way through to success. It always starts with real people. The ones who get up and walk the walk, instead of just talking the talk, sitting about in TV or internet armchairs or pub lounges all day, moaning about how they'd like things to be.

Take the musicians who sold millions of records with all those memorable tunes: talents like Lennon and McCartney, plotting and grafting, wanting it so bad it hurt; then becoming the greatest songwriting duo of all time. Actors, TV personalities and writers; men and women with stories to tell: McGovern, Bleasdale and Russell, hidden away in lofts, basements and cramped bedrooms for years. Scribbling away, harbouring an ache to be heard by the multitudes and to be out there. The football club founders: John Houlding and his manager Honest John McKenna, what would Liverpool FC be without those two noticing their football bootlaces and pulling them up so tightly that they kicked off a footballing dynasty virtually unrivalled in this country. Or George Mahon, an accountant, organist and his Reverend B.S. Chambers who wanted a football club run from St Domingo's church, and not Houlding's Anfield. Through their passionate endeavours we now have Everton FC, Dixie Dean and Tommy Lawton folklore, and one of the founding members of the football league. And what about hard-working, wheeling and dealing merchants with an entrepreneurial flair for business and finance; seeing their hopes and dreams flourish along the banks of the Mersey: Hornby (Meccano), Hargreaves (Matalan), Moores (Littlewoods), David Lewis (Lewis's), all people who wanted success and realized their business and financial dreams here in Liverpool.

Alongside the spirit of the city and that little bit of Mersey magic floating about in the air, what did they all have in common? Yeah, it was a passionate ambition to succeed... usually in their own chosen field where a prodigious or, often, only a modicum of talent lay. But whatever the quota of genius on board, they all quite simply took aim. And, undeterred, they continued to take aim until their ambitions were realized and success was there for all to see. Pulling themselves up by their own bootlaces they never stood around waiting for any EU handouts, or any help from in-fighting, small-minded councillors. No, they simply made the sacrifices needed to reach up for the stars, and allied to passion, doggedness and perseverance in abundance, they were up and out of the starting blocks. Given a sprinkling of talent, a good dose of Mersey air and passion and perseverance, and – away you go!

Do me and yourself a favour: don't wait round for any handouts or Culture money. You'll be worn out just waiting. It goes on house-brick size salaries, pie-in-the-sky ideas and second-hand underpants schemes. Leave them to in-fight, because like I've already told you, YOUR CITY NEEDS YOU NOW, more than it ever has before. It's make-or-break time for all you new writers, actors, musicians and entrepreneurs. Get on with it, don't give in, be a right pain in the arse by making the most of the fact that you're already lucky just to be born here. Only when YOU the Liverpool people take matters into YOUR own hands will the foundation stone be set for the next 800 years of Scouse-dom. The big personalities mentioned here helped put us on the map. But, in the end, it's Liverpool's warm-hearted street people who made and continue to make this city great. Me, I'm getting to it. Hope you are too. You know what... you just can't beat an angry, passionate Scouser!

If you're a local, get up and do something positive and in-the-face, and enjoy the year people... I aim to in whatever way I can. If you're a visiting Culturite, breathe our city in and buzz off the gaff, I do... daily. It's about the Mersey, about the people, about the humour. It's Liverpool!

Catch yer... Nicky Allt

At the end of January 2008 (first month of culture year) Liverpool City Council was named as the worst-run local authority by the CPA, the body that ranks councils. It demonstrated persistent political mismanagement, continually showed failure to make tough decisions, and the audit commission said it was the bottom of the league for the way it spent its money. At the same time Jason Harborow was offered a £230,000 payoff by the council to leave his position on the Cultural Company Board.

Selected Liverpool music to walk the city

⚜

DISC 1
1: The Beatles: I Feel Fine
2. The La's: Feeling
3. Shack: HMS Fable
4. Echo & the Bunnymen: The Killing Moon
5: Wah Heat: Better Scream
6: It's Immaterial: Driving Away From Home
7: The Real People: Rayners Lane
8: The Coral: Pass it on
9: Cast: Fine Time
10: Teardrop Explodes: Reward
11: Lightning Seeds: Pure
12: Cook Da Books: Piggy In The Middle 8
13: The Maybes: Rock'n Roll
14: Gerry & the Pacemakers: Don't let the sun catch you crying
15: Flock of Seagulls: I Ran
16: Paul McCartney: Every Night

DISC 2
1: The Icicle Works: When It All Comes Down
2: Elvis Costello: Red Shoes
3: Frankie Goes to Hollywood: Relax
4: Lotus Eaters: First Picture of You
5: The Christians: Forgotten Town
6: Billy Fury: A Wondrous Place
7: Space: Neighbourhood
8: John Power: Guiding Star
9: Deaf School: Room Service
10: The Farm: All Together Now
11: China Crisis: Black Man Ray

12: Liverpool Express: You Are My Love
13: George Harrison: My Sweet Lord
14: John Lennon: Working Class Hero
15: Ian McNabb: The New Golden Age
16: Pete Wylie: Heart as big as Liverpool

DISC 3
1: Shack: Cup of Tea
2: Teardrop Explodes: When I Dream
3: The La's: There She Goes
4: The Beatles: In My Life
5: Space: Female of the Species
6: China Crisis: King in a Catholic Style
7: The Christians: Hooverville
8: Elvis Costello: Oliver's Army
9: Ian McNabb: I'm A Genius
10: The Searchers: Needles and Pins
11: Echo & the Bunnymen: Back of Love
12: Badfinger: No Matter
13: George Harrison: Something
14: John Lennon: No. 9 Dream
15: Wings: Maybe I'm Amazed
16: Frankie: The Power of Love

Beatles, McNabb, Costello and the Bunnymen could've filled these discs alone; again, it's endless, so remember it's only a taster.

Thank you... and Goodnight